D0295528

What didn't happen next

Author acknowledgements:

The authors would like to thank Shari, Shiva, Susan (for keeping Peter and John out of the study), Peter and John (for keeping Susan out of the study), Jane Brand, Ken and Adele, Amanda Davis, Nicky Paris, Louise Dixon, 90 Minutes magazine and Panda (for the loan of his big red book).
'1966 And All That' was inspired by Robert Harley and John 'McGlashan' Docherty, so thanks to them too.

What didn't happen next

Nick Hancock's Alternative History of Football

Nick Hancock and Chris England

First published in Great Britain in 1997 by Chameleon Books
an imprint of André Deutsch Ltd
106 Great Russell Street
London WC1B 3LJ

André Deutsch Ltd is a subsidiary of VCI plc

www.vci.co.uk

Text copyright © Nick Hancock and Chris England 1997
1966 And All That © Chris England 1997

Design: Graham Black and Will Harvey for JMP Ltd
Picture research: Freddie Sloane for JMP Ltd

The right of Nick Hancock and Chris England to be identified as the authors of this
work has been asserted by them in accordance with the Copyright, Designs and
Patents act 1988

10 9 8 7 6 5 4 3 2 1

All rights reserved. This book is sold subject to the condition that it may not be
reproduced, stored in a retrieval system, or transmitted, in any form or by any means,
electronic, mechanical, photocopying, recording or otherwise, without the publisher's
prior consent

Printed and bound in Great Britain by Butler and Tanner, Frome and London

A catalogue record for this book is available from the British Library

ISBN 0 233 99291 X

Introduction

The Stylistics, whose singing style was based on Alan Ball's falsetto contribution to 'Back Home'.

FOOTBALL IS ALL ABOUT winners and losers. But mostly it's about losers. Only one team gets to win the League, only one team gets to win the Cup, and sometimes it's even the same team. In Scotland, only one team gets to win the League year after year after year, and more often than not wins the Cup as well.

The rest of us, the vast majority of football supporters everywhere, are left thinking about what might have been, if only . . .

If only. The saddest words in the English language, unless of course you are the Stylistics, who claimed in 1975 that ' "Na Na" is the saddest word', in a song that stank of 'time to fill on the album and only this shit to fill it with'. 'Na na' is only the saddest word when spoken by a grown man requesting a banana.

If only. A simple two-word phrase that encapsulates the flimsiness and futility of football ambition, the proximity of glory seemingly within reach but snatched away, hopes dashed, often by a matter of inches, or seconds, by the run of the ball, the want of a little bit of luck, or an ounce of composure at a crucial moment . . .

If only our keeper's hoofed clearance hadn't ricocheted from between our hapless full-back's shoulder blades, leaving the opposition forward with a tap-in two feet out with four seconds to go . . .

If only our forward hadn't thumped the ball with his eyes shut and both legs down the same hole of his shorts, so that his intended screaming thirty-yarder into the top corner actually sliced away embarrassingly to trickle up against the corner flag, without the pace to bounce out for a throw-in ...

If only the referee hadn't been waving at his mum in the stands as our winger was hacked down in the penalty area ...

Because often a match, a season, a whole career can turn on one moment, one incident, one mistake.

If Geoff Thomas had carried the ball forward for England against France in 1992, rounded the keeper, and scored with nonchalant ease, he could have fifty caps by now and be the England captain. Or perhaps not. As it was, of course, he scuffed the ball embarrassingly from forty yards out and never played for England again.

I**N THE 1997 FA CUP** semi-final between Chesterfield and Middlesbrough, you will remember, Middlesbrough were down to ten men. Midway through the second half Chesterfield's Jonathan Howard slammed a shot against the bar which clearly bounced out of the goal from behind the goal line, but the 'goal', which would have given his team a 3–1 lead, was mysteriously disallowed by a strange freak refereeing decision.

What Chesterfield fan hasn't subsequently wished he could just nip back in time and change that referee's call? But, of course, it is not as simple as that. He'd have to invent a time machine for a start, and parts aren't cheap. He wouldn't be able to afford his season ticket, so probably best to just forget it and learn to wallow in the tragedy of it all.

Anyway, once he changed that one little thing, then everything would be different from that moment on.

In *A Sound of Thunder* by Ray Bradbury, a time-travelling tourist visits the pre-

historic era. He is warned that under no circumstances may he leave the protected walkway for fear of interacting with the past, but, startled by the proximity of fearsome dinosaurs, he panics and gallops into the undergrowth. When he collects himself and returns to the safety of the walkway he is whisked forwards to a future that is utterly and irrevocably altered, and he finds, pressed to extinction on the sole of his shoe, a butterfly. This butterfly – who knows? – might have been the very one that, according to Chaos Theory, could cause a hurricane in China by flapping its wings in the Amazon rainforest.

So Chesterfield, going 3–1 up against ten men, might have gone on to win, but equally they might not. They might have become complacent, and Middlesbrough could have got a new lease of life, got some service to their international strike force, and pinched the game 4–3 at the death.

Or Chesterfield winning could have been a blessing in disguise for Boro, as, without the distraction of the FA Cup semi-final replay

Chesterfield's Sean Dyche celebrates inventing a time machine, nipping back to April 1997 and ripping off David Elleray's head.

Bobby Charlton shows Alan Ball how high a man of normal height can hoist the World Cup.

and final, they managed to get the three extra points that would have kept them up at Coventry's expense.

Then Coventry would have been relegated, and it would have been their expensive stars who would have left and scattered among the top clubs, or else spent the summer being linked with every club in Europe before returning humbled to their demoted team-mates, not Middlesbrough's. The consequences of that would reverberate through the next few seasons.

Once you start saying 'What if ...?' instead of 'If only ...', you begin to realise just how enormous the significance of individual moments in football can be.

The most extravagant example is probably the World Cup final of 1966. In extra time, as children ever since have been taught at their mother's breast, Alan Ball whipped in a cross

from the right wing. Geoff Hurst collected the ball and swivelled, smashing the ball against the bar and down on, near or over the line, depending on whether you are English, German, Scots or a Russian linesman.

Suppose that goal had not been given, and Germany had gone on to win the Cup. It is not overstating the case to say that the effects of this would have gone far beyond the confines of football alone. Such is the ludicrous importance still attached to this ancient win that even our national character would be different.

The changes to football history would have been dramatic enough. Subsequent England players would not have been burdened with the weight of unreasonable expectation and might have actually managed to qualify for a World Cup in the seventies.

Our inferiority complex with regard to Germany would have developed unchecked since the end of the Second World War. The sense that Germany has won the peace, economically and politically, is only held back with reference to 1966, for we have nothing more recent than that to taunt the Germans with (Eurovision Song Contest notwithstanding).

Without it we would have gradually become resigned to a place in Europe's second rank, a more pliable and docile member of the European Community, content to let the Germans and the French slug it out for the real supremacy. As it is, with that one flukish triumph to cling to as an example of what we are capable of, in the face of so many more recent reverses, we can still think of ourselves as a top European nation.

There is a theory, much loved by writers of science fiction, which suggests that a parallel universe exists where that reality is played out. Indeed, there are, apparently, an infinite number of parallel universes where reality forks and takes two paths at every pivotal moment, and so all possibilities are realised somewhere.

As in one episode of *Star Trek: The Next Generation*, which sends Lieutenant Worf flipping from one reality to another, gradually working his way further and further from the life he knows. He changes rank, finds a reality where he is married to Counsellor Troi, another where Captain Picard has been dead for several years, until a solution is found and he is returned to his own life. Luckily for him this happens before he discovers a parallel universe in which the crew of the 'Enterprise' use his forehead as a toast-rack.

It might be some small comfort to those of us dealing with defeat and disappointment on a regular basis to consider that somewhere out there is a parallel reality in which things work out the way we would have liked them to.

A reality in which Hitler never invaded Poland, and Stoke City won six successive championships between 1940 and 1945.

A reality in which Bob Wilson retired from football to begin his broadcasting career midway through Arsenal's 1971 FA Cup semi-final with Stoke, just walking off the pitch to interview himself about just what the hell he thought he was doing. The subsequent years being tormented by Bob's inane insights are happily traded for Stoke's 1971 Cup success and Arsenal's failure to win the double.

A reality in which Mark Hughes, just as he is about to connect with his sensational last-minute volley in the 1994 FA Cup semi-final, is flattened by half a ton of frozen urine dumped in error by a passing jumbo jet.

A reality in which Thomas Berthold, writhing in fake agony after a tackle by Paul Gascoigne in the 1990 World Cup semi-final, is eaten by a nearby Siberian tiger to the horror of the watching millions.

But we're in the realms of fantasy now. What we are considering in this book is what would have really happened if some of football's key moments had worked out the other way.

How things turn out when, instead of 'If only ...' we say, 'What if ...?'

A Siberian tiger and Thomas Berthold (hidden).

If... Gordon Banks had played against West Germany in León, 14 June 1970 *then...* there would have been no such thing as Thatcherism

Banksie breaks the squad high-jump record using the new-fangled Fosbury Flop.

IN 1970 ALF RAMSEY'S England team went to Mexico to defend the World Cup as one of the tournament favourites. Like Ramsey himself, many critics believed his squad to be even stronger than the one which had won the trophy four years earlier. And much stronger than the only previous British squad to win the trophy on foreign soil. You know, the one Dennis Waterman played for in 1912, with the long shorts.

Gordon Banks, of Stoke City, was undoubt-edly the world's finest goalkeeper, as he was to demonstrate conclusively during the course of the tournament. His positioning, agility and handling were such that he presented a formidable obstacle to the best the world's strikers had to offer, and his good sense appalled journalists obsessed with the notion that 'All goalkeepers are crazy'.

In Ramsey's 4–4–2 system there was no place for wingers, and so the full backs, Keith Newton and Terry Cooper, were expected to overlap and provide crosses. The heart of the defence was captain Bobby Moore, at the very peak of his game, with Everton's Brian Labone alongside him.

In midfield Ramsey retained three of the heroes of 1966. Bobby Charlton was nearing the end of his magnificent career, Alan Ball and Martin Peters were well-established

England coach driver Ken Bracket shows Sir Alf where he can stick his sausages.

internationals, and Alan Mullery of Spurs completed the quartet. A foursome whose guile, wisdom and soccer nous seemed fated to make them the next generation of great managers. Which just goes to show that fate knows fuck all.

Up front Geoff Hurst had matured into one of the world's top forwards, seemingly unhampered by his habit of puffing his cheeks out at the moment of striking the ball – a nervous habit resulting from a childhood birthday cake incident – and he was partnered by the squat figure of Frannie Lee.

This powerful team was not at all popular in Mexico. The victory of four years earlier was seen as the result of home advantage and poor refereeing. The locals were offended by Alf Ramsey's aloof and distant attitude, but his unfortunate manner meant that he was often misunderstood, and in fact when he appeared aloof and distant in truth he was merely arrogant and a long way off.

Brazil, on the other hand, were lionised and mobbed wherever they went, and they cultivated a large local following with gifts and charm. At their training sessions they would spend time having photographs taken with local children and doing tricks to entertain them. England, widely regarded as Brazil's main challengers for the trophy, were cast as the villains, and seemingly could do nothing right.

WHILE IN BOGOTÁ en route to Mexico after a warm-up friendly, Bobby Moore was scandalously accused of stealing a bracelet from a jeweller's store in the team hotel. Despite the thinness of the evidence against him, Moore was held for four days before being released on bail. Further charges against Frannie Lee for smuggling fruit, and Allan Clarke for running a Colombian brothel, later turned out to be journalistic scare stories.

Then Jeff Astle had to be helped off the plane bringing the England team to Mexico.

Apparently he was rattled by turbulence on the flight and drank too much. It's happened to the best of us. I was rattled by turbulence only last week at a mate's wedding.

All this led to England being labelled drunks and thieves by the local press, which was bizarre considering there were no Arsenal players in the squad.

And there was nowhere to hide once they arrived in Guadalajara, because their hotel was secluded only in the Piccadilly Circus sense of the word, leaving them easy prey to prank wake-up calls and cacophonous all-night street noise.

Nevertheless England were expected to show well once the tournament started, not least by Prime Minister Harold Wilson. He was relying on the 'feel-good' factor that winning performances by England would bring about to help him clinch the General Election he had called for Thursday 18 June, the day after the semi-finals.

England began their defence of the Cup against Romania. To mark the occasion of England's first appearance on colour television, they played in all white. The game was decided by a single goal from Puffer Hurst, who took a cross from Alan Ball past one defender and nutmegged the Romanian keeper, Adamache.

Then came Brazil, in a match that was billed as a rehearsal for the final by an English press that has learned nothing in the intervening years about tempting fate and counting chickens while in their pre-hatched state. The game kicked off at midday to accommodate European television requirements – i.e., so it didn't clash with *On the Buses* – and consequently took place in a sweltering 98 degrees.

Its most memorable moment came after eleven minutes. Jairzinho crossed from the right over Banks, who was covering the near post. Pelé rose above Mullery, and headed the ball hard down towards the other corner of the net, and in that heart-

beat everyone in the Jalisco Stadium prepared to celebrate a goal. As the ball reached the goal line, however, Banks, scrambling desperately across, managed to flick the ball up and over the bar to safety. In that instant Banks marked himself out as not only the world's foremost keeper, but also as England's key player.

The goal that won the game in the fifty-ninth minute was made by Tostão and Pelé and scored by Jairzinho. England did, however, create several chances, the best of which was squandered by Jeff Astle – added to the squad at the eleventh hour to bolster the baritone section on 'Back Home' – and they joined Brazil in the quarter finals after a 1–0 win over Czechoslovakia, Allan Clarke scoring from the penalty spot.

Feb 1971. Banks suffers a surprise recurrence of Montezuma's Revenge during a League match against Chelsea.

'No, honest, I'm alright Boss ...'

ENGLAND'S OPPONENTS in León would be the West Germans, who had finished top of Group Four thanks in no small part to seven goals from *'Der Bomber'*, Gerd Muller – so-called for his predilection for jumping into the pool and splashing innocent holidaymakers.

It would be tough, with the Germans out for revenge, but it seemed tougher still when Gordon Banks became ill the day before the match. The fact that England had brought with them 140 lb of beefburgers, 400 lb of sausages, 300 lb of frozen fish and ten cases of tomato ketchup, and that no one else in the party fell ill, led to suspicions that Banks had been nobbled. But then again, the night before he had eaten 140 lb of beefburgers, 400 lb of sausages, 300 lb of frozen fish, and ten cases of tomato ketchup.

However, the keeper proclaimed himself fit on the morning of the game, only to suffer what was politely described as a relapse, but what can only have been Banksie cutting short the phrase, 'No, honest, I'm all right boss ...' to make a mad dash for the crapper. Ramsey considered risking it, but the referee's insistence that Banks would have to wear white shorts convinced the manager that the risk wasn't worth taking.

'Now wash your hands!' quips referee Doug Bald.

SO IT WAS THAT Peter 'The Cat' Bonetti took his place between the sticks for the biggest game of his life, and it wasn't to be a happy experience. It wasn't all his fault. His insistence on being called 'The Cat' had backfired on him, and he had been forced to spend the previous three weeks quarantined in a cat basket in Acapulco.

England stormed into a two-goal lead through Mullery, Peters and Ball – one apiece for Mullery and Peters and none for Ball – and with twenty minutes to go Ramsey was preparing to substitute Charlton to save him for the semi-final.

Franz Beckenbauer played a graceful one–two off Francis Lee's wedding tackle and advanced on goal. Mullery forced him wide, and his shot seemed to carry little threat. It was good enough to bamboozle Bonetti,

though, who dived clean over it as it bobbled into the net.

Nine minutes later Bonetti was caught again by a flukish but eminently preventable back-headed goal by Uwe Seeler, and the match reached the end of 90 minutes with the score at 2–2. In extra time the Germans summoned up a third, scored from about eight inches by *Der Bomber*, with the tired England defence nowhere to be seen.

It was a shattering defeat. Banks was watching the match from his sick bed, and the delay on the broadcast meant that when his dejected team-mates returned to the hotel he believed the score to be 2–0 and thought they were winding him up.

We were out of the World Cup, and gone for ever was the chance of a World Cup final being decided by goals from Peters and Lee.

But what if...
Banks had been fit?

ENGLAND, BUOYED BY the presence of their brilliant and dependable goalie, started confidently and quickly gained the upper hand. Neither keeper was tested, however, before the thirty-first minute, when Mullery played a one–two with Lee, and another with Newton, meeting the full-back's cross eight yards out and sweeping it past Maier for his first international goal. West Germany struggled to respond, as Cooper was dominating their main outlet, the winger Libuda, and half-time arrived with England still a goal up.

Early in the second half England extended their lead. Keith Newton galloped down the wing and sent over a deep cross which Peters slipped in behind Berti Vogts to squeeze home for two–nil.

Up to this point Banks had not been seriously tested, and the England management could have been forgiven for thinking that Peter Bonetti could have handled anything the Germans had created, had Banks been too ill to take part.

Helmut Schoen withdrew the ineffective Libuda and sent on Grabowski, another winger. The heat and effort had drained Cooper, and Grabowski soon found he could threaten the England goal. The Germans began to take control.

On sixty-nine minutes Franz Beckenbauer, 'Der Kaiser', picked up the ball, played a wall pass off Frannie Lee's packet, and sent a low shot towards goal. Banks was down early, and winced as the ball thumped into

his belly, but he managed to hold on, both to the ball and his breakfast.

Thereafter the England defence held firm, and although a scrambled goal from Muller with five minutes to go sparked frantic pressure from the Germans, a breakaway goal by Hurst in the dying seconds finished them off. Some people ran on to the pitch, thinking it was all over, and very soon after that it was.

THE TEAMS

ENGLAND
Banks, Newton, Cooper, Mullery, Labone, Moore, Ball, Lee, R.Charlton, Hurst, Peters.

WEST GERMANY
Maier, Schnellinger, Vogts, Fichtel, Hottges, Beckenbauer, Overath, Seeler, Libuda, Muller, Lohr.

Banks is narrowly beaten, despite having his hands tied together.

After the match Alf Ramsey was warmly congratulated for his key substitutions, which had proved vital. Colin Bell had subdued Beckenbauer, and the tiring Charlton still had something in the tank for the semi-final, while Hunter had defended manfully in the last minutes after replacing Peters, clearing one goal-bound Seeler header off the line.

WEST GERMANY	**1**
Muller 85	
ENGLAND	**3**
Mullery 31, Peters 49,	
Hurst 90	

IN THE SEMI-FINAL England met Italy in a tight game, both defences stifling any attempts at attacking play. With ten minutes to go the game's best chance fell to substitute Jeff Astle, who redeemed himself for his earlier blunder against Brazil and slotted home the winner.

Brazil beat Uruguay 3–1 in the other semi-final to set up the expected 'Dream Final'. This was confusing to me as a seven-year old, because my dream final was Stoke versus my sisters' girls school. Jimmy Greaves, working as an ITV pundit for the first time, was sacked for punching the air and making a Red Indian whooping noise when he learned of Alf Ramsey's controversial decision to drop Hurst.

The final lived up to expectations, with Moore and Banks in top form holding the Brazilians until half-time. In the second half, however, Pelé scored with a spectacular header, and made another for Jairzinho.

Allan Clarke pulled one back, but Pelé set up a glorious third for overlapping full back Carlos Alberto, and Brazil had won the World Cup for the third time.

(Above) After the so-called 'Dream Final', Carlos Alberto lifts the trophy, and (Far right) two great players and sportsmen pay tribute to each other. They would next meet on the set of *Escape to Victory*.

Banks went from humble tea-boy to England's No 1.

● England's dramatic quarter final victory over West Germany, and their semi-final defeat of Italy, brought about a national feel-good factor and a sense of optimism and anticipation. This contributed, as Harold Wilson had calculated, to a comfortable Labour victory in the General Election of 18 June, two days before the final.

● Wilson himself was fond of saying, 'Have you ever noticed how England only ever win the World Cup under a Labour government?' – not the most pithy of catchphrases – and there were enough superstitious football fans in the electorate to ensure a Labour working majority of thirty.

● Defeated Tory leader Edward Heath staved off a leadership challenge from upstart Margaret Thatcher, who made herself very unpopular within the Conservative Party and was removed from the Shadow Cabinet.

● Heath had planned to take the UK into the Common Market in 1973, but Wilson instead offered the country a referendum, and abided by its decisive 'No to Europe' result. Colin Stein, of Coventry City, was particularly gutted, missing out as he did on the strongly mooted 3 v 6 Common Market entry celebration game.

● After the Conservative Party's narrow victory in the 1975 General Election, Harold Wilson announced his retirement, and Denis Healey became Labour leader in opposition to Prime Minister Edward Heath.

● Margaret Thatcher, infuriated by the moderate centre politics of both the main parties, left the Conservative Party to form her own, breakaway, outfit. Their policies of mass privatisation of public utilities, restrictive legislation to curb the power of the unions, worship of market forces, mistrust of Europe, and a pre-emptive military strike against Argentina, were seen as extreme, unworkable, and frankly barking mad. She became an increasingly marginal figure in politics, and began a new career as a team captain on *Call My Bluff*. Here she flourished, genuinely unaware of the definitions of words such as democracy, freedom and compassion.

● Meanwhile, after five years of Heath and Healey arguing over the dispatch box, Mike Yarwood entered the 1980s as Britain's top entertainer. He turned down the opportunity to move his successful BBC programme to ITV, following in the footsteps of Morecambe and Wise and Sooty – if Sooty can be said to have footsteps – and revealed that he would have been tempted to turn to drink if only things weren't going so remarkably well.

● Denis Healey moved into 10 Downing Street, followed by Michael Heseltine, Neil Kinnock, John Major and Tony Blair, as the two main parties took turn and turn about presiding over a country whose Health Service, Welfare State, coal industry and transport network were the envy of the world in general and the ailing Britain-free European Community in particular.

● Bobby Charlton retired after the World Cup final with 108 caps, a record later equalled by Bobby Moore, and surpassed by Peter Shilton. Shilton missed out on the 1970 World Cup squad despite featuring in 'Back Home', the number one hit single, and in the Esso World Cup coin collection.

● Sir Alf Ramsey became Lord Ramsey of Ipswich in the 1971 New Year's Honours List, for services to the sausage industry.

● Losing to England in the World Cup twice in succession gave the West German players and supporters a real inferiority complex about England. They began to feel England were their jinx team, and complained that the English were arrogant as a nation.

● English holidaymakers strutted confidently about the Mediterranean resorts, getting up early to reserve sunbeds with large Union Jack towels, while their German counterparts huddled in the bars out of the sun muttering about how they won the World Cup in 1954, and that for long periods the war had seemed to be going their way.

● England's psychological hold over West Germany was crucial when the teams next met in a major tournament, the European Championships of 1972. Despite being outplayed by a German team in which Günter Netzer was outstanding, England still managed to win the game, and a draw in the return leg saw England through.

● England lost the semi-final to Belgium in Antwerp. The Belgians went on to beat the USSR in the final.

● The West Germans were badly rattled by their failure to win the Championship, and spent the two years leading to the 1974 World Cup changing their line-up in search of a successful side.

● Despite home advantage, they were unconvincing in the World Cup finals, and were edged out when New Zealand and El Salvador contrived a draw to eliminate them at the group stage on goal difference. The Germans cried 'Foul!', but since this is German for spatchcock it was to no avail. Johan Cruyff's Holland beat Poland in the World Cup final in Munich, and, as Barry Davies famously commented, there was clog-dancing in the streets of Nijmegen that night.

● German football went into a decline from which it has yet to recover. German youths drifted into other sports, and there are now German world champions in octopush, korfball and Galaxian, while their pin up boy is world diving champion Jürgen Klinsmann.

● England failed to qualify for the 1974 World Cup, but the manager's place in history was secure, and he retired with the knowledge that wherever football was played the name of Sir Ralph Rumsey would be remembered.

Stockport County's most successful triallist ever does an impromptu Alex Ferguson impression while still dressed as Willie Thorne.

If... Tomaszewski had been a clown then... Cloughie would have been England manager

JIMMY GREAVES SAID that if Kevin Hector's header had gone into the net it would have changed the course of English football history.

Hector made his England début in bizarre circumstances on 17 October 1973. With England drawing against Poland 1–1 in a match that they had to win to qualify for the 1974 World Cup, Sir Alf Ramsey turned to his subs bench.

'Kevin, get stripped,' he said, and quick as a flash Kevin Keegan jumped up and took off his tracksuit. 'Oh, not you!' Ramsey barked. 'The other one.' Kevin Hector duly replaced Martin Chivers, with 100 seconds to save the day for England.

(What isn't widely known is that Ramsey believed that Derek Kevan, the clumsy West Brom star of the fifties, was also on the bench, and he hadn't intended for Hector to play either.)

Tough though the task was, Hector came closer than anyone to getting the vital goal,

his close range header from England's twenty-third corner cleared desperately off the line. Moments later the final whistle went, and England had failed.

On the face of it England's qualifying group had seemed a straightforward one. Opponents Wales were a familiar bunch, and Poland were an unknown quantity – although we suspected there'd be eleven of them – not particularly highly rated by the football world, and they had never before beaten England.

Still, there's a first time for everything, and Poland's 2–0 win in Chorzow, together with England's lame 1–1 draw with Wales at Wembley, meant that a draw in this last match would send Poland through.

England were confident, however, and in good form. In their previous Wembley appearance, a friendly against Austria, they had scored seven without reply, and Ramsey's team was unchanged.

The pundits were equally upbeat, Brian

Arthur Askey
and Nana
Mouskouri join
the celebrations
as Poland
qualify for the
1974 World Cup.

Clough singled out the goal-keeper, Jan Tomaszewski, calling him 'a clown', and his assistant at Derby, Peter Taylor, went further, saying that the whole Polish team were 'donkeys'.

CLOUGH WAS THEN a full-time TV pundit, having walked out of Derby County on the morning of the England–Poland match. He had criticised some of his Derby players in a newspaper column, claiming they were not giving 100 per cent for the club because of the imminent international. The Derby chairman had demanded that Clough relinquish his burgeoning media career, so he resigned.

THE TEAMS

ENGLAND
Shilton, Madeley, Hughes, Bell, McFarland, Hunter, Currie, Channon, Chivers (Hector), Clarke, Peters.

POLAND
Tomaszewski, Szymanowski, Gorgon, Musial, Bulzacki, Kasparczak, Lato, Cmikiewicz, Deyna, Domarski, Gadocha.

Straight from the kick-off England laid siege to the Poland goal. Channon hit the post, Currie headed over the top. Tomaszewski, aided by his springy long boots that had been run over by an old jalopy moments earlier, dived to turn aside a Bell shot, then made saves from Clarke and Channon with help from his revolving bow tie and little flaps of ginger hair which bounced up and down.

Half-time arrived with no score. Then, after twelve minutes of further England pressure, Poland broke down the left. Hunter failed to intercept Lato, allowing the ball to slip under his foot, and Shilton failed to intercept Domarski's shot, allowing the ball to slip under his body.

(Left) Mike Channon inches wide ... and that's just his sideburns. (Above) Shilton would unnerve his defence by insisting on playing hide-and-seek during important internationals.

Although England equalised with a Clarke penalty shortly after, the 'clown' held England at bay. His own team-mates were exasperated with him at one point, when the trainer ran on to treat an injury, only to find that his water bucket was full of little bits of confetti, but otherwise Tomaszewski – 'Toto' – was the hero.

IN THE AFTERMATH of England's failure Ramsey was sacked. Joe Mercer took over as caretaker manager – a role similar to Ramsey's but with additional responsibility for looking after everyone's spare keys. He replaced Ramsey's functionalism with a more carefree attacking style, giving débuts to Keith Weller, Frank Worthington and Alec Lindsay, and bringing on Trevor Brooking, Martin Dobson, Mike Pejic, Stan Bowles and Dave Watson, who had all made their first appearances in Ramsey's last international against Portugal.

In the summer Don Revie was appointed. He duly failed to qualify for the European Championships of 1976, and left with England all but out of the 1978 World Cup, moving to Saudi Arabia to introduce sock tags and carpet bowls to the Middle East.

Poland, meanwhile, had a lovely time at the World Cup finals in Germany, where they finished third and purchased the tracksuits that the Polish team still wear to this day. Gregorz Lato finished as the tournament's top scorer.

But what if... Hector's last minute header had crept in?

(Right) Brian Clough in only his pants.

ONE HUNDRED SECONDS TO GO. *Derby County's striker Kevin Hector enters the fray. From a corner he glances a header goalwards, and a Polish defender strains to keep it out. His clearance deflects off Tomaszewski's unicycle and loops crazily back into the net. There is bare-ly time to restart before the final whistle blows, and England scrape into the World Cup finals as the jammiest of the fourteen qualifiers.*

ENGLAND   2
Clarke (pen) 64,
Hector 90
POLAND   1
Domarski 57

● In the friendlies before the World Cup Ramsey resists the temptation to experiment with his formation. Channon, Clarke and Hector will be his main strikers, and the Derby man becomes Sir Alf's lucky mascot.

● The press camp outside the new England star's residence and print photographs under the rather obvious headline 'Hector's House'. This annoys his neighbours, singer Kiki Dee and actress Zsa Zsa Gabor, who have moved to Derby for a bit of peace and quiet.

● England are drawn in Group 4 with Argentina, Italy and Haiti. As in 1970

England suffer from a lack of fire-power, and although they perform creditably in achieving 0–0 draws with Argentina and Italy, the 0–0 draw they play with Haiti means that England are eliminated. Papa Doc Duvalier, Haiti's leader, is elated, however, saying: 'No longer will the English confuse us with Eric Sykes's screen sister.'

● Ramsey is criticised heavily for the inflexibility of his tactics. His rigid adherence to a 4–4–2 system in a tournament in which Holland demonstrated 'total football' to the world is damaging enough, but persistently bringing Hector on as sub with two minutes to go in every match is his downfall.

● Sir Alf recognises that he has gone as far as he can as England manager, and resigns from the job on England's return from West Germany.

● The Football Association consider a number of alternatives, including Gordon Jago, Jimmy Bloomfield and Gordon Milne, but in the end they turn to Brian Clough in an attempt to shake some life back into the English game. Clough has been managing Third Division Brighton since leaving Derby County, the 1972 League Champions, and the FA are especially impressed by his perspicacity in correctly identifying the clownish nature of Jan Tomaszewski.

● Don Revie, the Leeds United manager, is bitter about being overlooked, especially as he had 'greased all the right palms', but he steers Leeds to the European Cup in 1975. He subsequently finds it emotionally difficult to replace his old favourites at Elland Road and in 1977 he suddenly leaves to take a lucrative post at MI5, where they have long been jealous of his dossier-making skills.

● Clough embarks on a rebuilding programme, although he makes it clear that Peter Shilton is to be his number one choice as keeper, despite the much-touted rival claims of Liverpool's Ray Clemence. Shilton eventually retires in 1990 with a world record 179 caps.

● Clough builds a side that plays with flair and freedom. Shilton, Nish, Todd, McFarland and Watson form a reliable defence, Worthington and Keegan are his first choice strikers, while in midfield, Hudson, Tueart and Brooking are controversially joined by new England captain John 'Scotty' McGovern.

● England qualify for the European Championship in 1976, where they unluckily lose a thrilling final on penalties to West Germany.

● Don Revie suggests that, had he been made England manager, he would have had a get-together with eighty of England's top players, to let them all know that the England door was open. Clough goes to the pub with John McGovern.

● Clough has enemies in the FA (not least the evil Moriarty) who are annoyed by his lack of respect for their opinions and his hard-line refusal to pick Leeds United players he describes as 'tainted'. They niggle and provoke him as England's qualifying games for the 1978 World Cup get under way.

● Clough accuses the FA of wanting him to fail, citing their crazy timetabling of the qualifying programme and their refusal to cancel the Saturday League programme before crucial internationals that they have scheduled for Sunday afternoons.

● The final split comes, however, when the FA refuse to sanction a mooted set of Esso commemorative coins, which would have had a big one the size of a saucer right in the middle featuring a representation of Brian Clough as Christ at Calvary. Clough walks out and England, in disarray, miss out on the 1978 World Cup finals. West Ham's Ron Greenwood is the new England manager. Barabbas is freed.

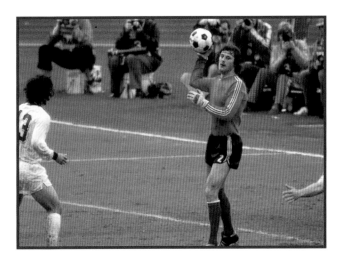

(Above) The World Cup's newly painted posts were a cleaning nightmare for keepers prone to leaning against them when the action lulled. (Below) Elvis fan Frank Worthington was seldom 'Lonesome Tonight' in this outfit.

If... George Best had been pig-ugly ...would we even have heard of Pelé?

GEORGE BEST WAS BORN IN 1946 into a Belfast that was impoverished, austere and, as far as we can tell from pictures of that era, still in black and white. He emerged from this monochrome upbringing, however, to become one of the most colourful and talented characters the twin worlds of football and brewing have ever known.

God bestows gifts like those he gave George Best rarely indeed. In painting there's Rolf Harris and in music, of course, Robson and Jerome. In football history perhaps only Best among Europeans can stand comparison with Pelé and Maradona.

His astonishing performances in the 1968 European Cup campaign are all the more impressive when you remember that he was barely out of his teens, and he dominated English football right up to the shock retirement in 1972.

It hurts me to say how brilliant he was, because I do not have much love for the club he played for, but truly great players transcend even the most deep-rooted prejudices. It was the same with Mickey Droy.

Best arrived in Manchester just as the so-called swinging sixties were getting under way. Apart from a brief bout of homesickness – perhaps Manchester was just too colourful for him – Best was a model apprentice and young pro. He was modest, hard-working and brilliant.

He was also good-looking, a pin-up boy with his lithe frame, blue eyes and jet black hair, and he was the first footballing superstar. He attracted the sort of attention usually reserved for pop idols, and indeed was known in the sixties as the fifth Beatle. Possibly this initially came about because

'Here it is, darling, come and get it!' George Best was an un-conventional lollipop man.

Best's legendary ball control skills included levitation by hypnosis.

he was mistaken for Pete Best, the fourth Beatle. Strictly speaking, of course, Ringo was the fifth Beatle. Which is to say he was the second fifth Beatle, after Stuart Sutcliffe but before George Martin. And Brian Epstein.

With success on the field came a playboy lifestyle off it. Best loved to go to nightclubs dressed in a tie-dye T-shirt and slacks and would spend all evening impressing Miss Worlds by making a pyramid of champagne glasses.

Matt Busby seemed to know how to handle the boy-genius so that things didn't get out of hand, and Best won two championships, the European Cup, Footballer of the Year and European Footballer of the Year in 1968. After Busby retired, however, Best began to believe his own publicity and became distracted by the world outside football, the

peripheral, glamorous, partying, drinking, society world.

At the age of twenty-six – coincidentally the same age at which Alan Hudson's career effectively finished with a tragic transfer to the USA – Best turned his back on the game. No player before had had to deal with the pressures and the limelight that surrounded the Irishman. There were comebacks, with Fulham, Hibernian and New York Cosmos, but essentially Georgie never learned to handle the twin careers of footballer and playboy.

As the crowds would rightly sing, Georgie Best was a superstar, although there's no actual proof that he ever carried a handbag or wore a bra.

Best himself theorised that his looks had been a hindrance to realising his potential as a footballer, saying: 'If I'd been ugly, you'd never have heard of Pelé.'

But what if... George Best had *really* been ugly?

THE JOKES ABOUT the unfortunate George Best abound. When he was a baby he was so ugly that the neighbours used to peer at him and say to his mum: 'Well... What a lovely pram.' His dad used to tie a lamb chop to his leg to get the dog to play with him.

Best's ugliness has overshadowed a long and satisfactory career as a ball-winning midfielder who sat on the Manchester United bench a record 431 times as understudy first to Nobby Stiles, then Ian Ure, Steve James, Brian Greenhoff, Mickey Thomas and Remi Moses.

Best has shouldered the burden of his extreme ugliness with great good humour. He even has a picture on his wall of the famous occasion at Stoke when the whole of the home crowd turned to face away from the pitch when he came on as substitute.

If there is any bitterness it is with FIFA, who denied him the chance to add to his solitary Northern Ireland cap by banning him from international football on the grounds that '...being as ugly as Best is constitutes continued ungentlemanly conduct.' Despite a petition signed by Rudi Voller, Jim Leighton, Peter Beardsley and Iain Dowie this unprecedented ban was never lifted.

'It is something I have learned to live with,' said Best, dabbing one of the

One picture.
One player.
Three tongues.

numerous running sores on his face. 'Do you know, I've never been in SHOOT, and until I realised what was going on the club would always give me the wrong date or location for the team photograph.'

Football has spared George Best from a

'Cover those girls up, George. Lend them your tie.'

potentially miserable life. Although he left school with few qualifications – teachers were unwilling to invigilate his examinations after a young maths teacher went mad trying to calculate the number of George's spots – he had an advantage when it came to being scouted as a young footballer.

Most scouts couldn't bring themselves to watch him more than once, and they made hasty judgements softened by the sympathy they felt for the boy they dubbed 'Carcrash'.

Many with strong stomachs who saw him play often in those early days maintain that he could have been quite a player, of

a different type altogether from the timorous percentage player we know he became. They saw in him a creator, an entertainer, a virtuoso even. Ironically, before he got his jaw fixed and a glandular problem sorted out he was callously nicknamed 'The Wizard of Dribble'.

The virtuoso thrives on confidence, however, and needs the impudence to exert his superiority over lesser mortals, while George was always humble and self-effacing. Matt Busby says it took him three years at United to rid Best of the habit of saying 'Sorry' whenever he dispossessed anyone.

None the less he was always a steady performer for United, and popular in his way. He even flirted briefly with a stage career in a local production of The Rocky Horror Show, *a publicity push for which led to his now infamous appearance on* Wogan. *The famous Irishman staggered on, obviously drunk, mumbling incoherently, but when he caught sight of George Best, sobered up immediately.*

Best hung up his boots at the age of thirty-six after Northern Ireland's World Cup campaign in 1982. He would have liked the chance to appear on the world stage, but FIFA, mindful of the global television audience and the fact that there might be children watching, would not relax their long-standing ban.

The United faithful will always have a place in their hearts for this unique, quiet Irishman, whose abstinence, hard work, good manners, loyalty and genuine humility won't stand in the way of his being remembered as the only professional foot-baller to have described Ian Rush as 'a bit of a looker'.

And there will always be the apocryphal story of the hotel porter who came into Best's hotel room one afternoon to find the Irishman sprawled on the big double bed with a bottle of ginger ale, watching Going for Gold *with Olympic pentathlete Mary Peters.*

He looked around, clearly awe-struck, and asked plaintively, 'Mary, Mary, where did it all go wrong for you?'

So I think, on balance, George, we would have heard of Pelé if you'd been pig ugly. Which thank the Lord you weren't, sir.

George smuggles Rodney Marsh into a game under his coat.

'Mary, Mary, where did it all go wrong?'

If••• Panenka had missed his winning penalty in the 1976 European Championship final shootout

THE 1976 EUROPEAN CHAMPIONSHIP final in Belgrade was between West Germany (naturally) and Czechoslovakia. The Czechs' victims en route included England and Wales in the qualifying tournament, the USSR, and a Dutch side that was between World Cup finals and featured the likes of Cruyff, Neeskens, Rep and Rensenbrinck. The Germans had muscled by Spain and the hosts Yugoslavia.

Czechoslovakia, at first, seemed to be running away with the final. Svehlik and Dobias gave them a two-goal lead, but Müller pegged them back to 2–1 at half-time. A second half equaliser from Holzenbein, whose name, pleasingly, translates literally as 'Wooden leg', took the game to extra time, and subsequently a penalty shoot-out.

Seven penalties hit the target, and then Uli Hoeness blasted his kick over the crossbar. This left Panenka needing to score with his attempt to give Czechoslovakia the title.

Many players in this high-pressure position would just pick a spot and kick the ball as hard as they could with their eyes shut, but Panenka was cooler than that. He trotted up as though about to smash the ball, sending Maier diving desperately to his right,

then... Gary Lineker would be England's top goalscorer of all time

then just dinked it into the net where the German goalkeeper had been standing.

Sixteen years later Gary Lineker was nearing the end of a splendid England career as he lined up to face Brazil in a friendly at Wembley. He had announced that he would retire after the 1992 European Championships in Sweden, and with forty-eight goals from his seventy-five internationals he was just one goal behind Bobby Charlton's all-time England scoring record. Clinching at least a share of the record seemed a formality, with another friendly, against Finland, to come, and then the Euro 92 finals themselves. England were awarded a penalty against Brazil, and Lineker stepped up to take it. The nation and the Wembley crowd prepared to salute the record-equalling goal. Now when Lineker had taken penalties before for England, against Cameroon in Italia 90, he had (apparently) thought of his brother's bar in Tenerife and blasted the ball as hard as he could. And that seemed to go all right.

He had, however, scored a penalty Panenka-style in a recent cup tie against Nottingham Forest, and decided that he would reach this momentous landmark with another cool dink.

In the event Lineker stubbed his toe on the turf, and the ball dribbled embarrassingly towards the Brazilian keeper, who simply bent down and picked it up, not even dignifying the effort with a pretend dive. The crowd sighed, but believed that the forty-ninth goal – and even a fiftieth – would inevitably come before the Lineker boots finally reached the Lineker peg. Sadly, of course, he never had as good a chance again and remains second on the list. And that stubbed toe was never quite right again.

(Left) The greatest penalty of all time. (Above) The shite-ist penalty of all time.

If... Scotland really had made it to dreamland

then... **Keith Burkinshaw could have been president of Argentina**

AFTER THEIR PERFORMANCES in the 1974 World Cup, Scotland's standing on the international stage was at its highest. Obviously they hadn't made it to the second phase, but they didn't have to, it was still Scotland's most impressive World Cup performance ever. They had been eliminated unbeaten from the finals on goal difference, and first Tommy Docherty then Willie Ormond had made them a force to be reckoned with. They certainly emerged with more credit than the tournament's official mascots Tip and Tap – the second crappiest double act in football history after Graham Taylor and Lawrie McMenemy.

Despite being drawn in the same qualifying group as European champions Czechoslovakia, Scotland approached the 1978 World Cup with a good deal of optimism.

During the qualifying competition, however, Ormond, like Docherty before him, balked at the money he was offered by the SFA and stepped down to return to club management, at Hearts.

The SFA, pleasingly conforming to the national stereotype – the one about Scotsmen being stingy, not the one about them being incoherent rambling drunks – chose to

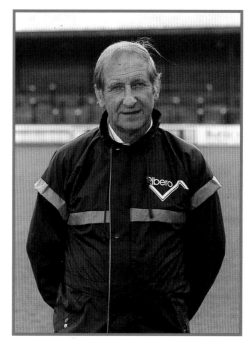

(Far left) And Scotland are in dreamland ... while (Left) their manager is in cloud-cuckoo land.

Joe Jordan played for A C Milan. But then so did Luther Blissett.

ignore the saying: 'if you pay peanuts you get monkeys', and employed the King of the Swingers himself: one Mr Ally MacLeod.

'It's Argentina or Siberia', he declared on taking over, displaying a fine sense of direction which initially masked his lack of credentials for the job. These amounted to ten years in charge of part-timers Ayr United – so that's about six years of proper experience, presumably – followed by eighteen months as boss at Aberdeen where he won the League Cup. Initial misgivings were hushed, though, as Scotland won their last two qualifying games to top their group.

First they beat the Czechs 3–1 at Hampden, and then, in a match featuring a fine 'What if...?' moment, they accounted for Wales at Anfield. With ten minutes to go and the score nil–nil, a high ball into the Welsh area was clearly handled. The French referee thought the guilty man was David Jones of Wales and awarded a penalty, whereas the replays showed incontrovertibly that it had been Joe Jordan.

This was a particularly savage double blow for Jones. Not only robbed of a place in the World Cup finals, but also mistaken for Joe Jordan. That's the sort of blow that can destroy a man.

Jones could console himself with the thought that if the Welsh had managed to force a win, and had gone to Argentina as the sole British team to qualify, they surely couldn't have cocked it up as badly as the Scots did.

Once England's failure to qualify was certain, the full glare of the British media turned on the Scots, and Ally MacLeod in particular. The self-appointed national messiah replied with fine xenophobic triumphalism. He mocked the English for missing the boat, and made Scotland out to be realistic contenders for the trophy itself. The English had to bite their tongues and hope that MacLeod was all mouth and no trousers. It was difficult to be sure, on

account of the fact that his mouth was so big you couldn't tell whether he was wearing trousers or not.

Whatever, he whipped up a mood of frantic optimism, and hundreds of fans – Ally's Tartan Army – spent their life savings travelling down to Argentina to share in the expected glory.

MacLeod was especially scathing about English football, despite the fact that the bulk of his squad played in it, and that England had just beaten Scotland at Hampden in the 1978 Home Internationals. After this defeat MacLeod sent his team on a lap of honour to rub qualification in the faces of the English, but to parade in this fashion, especially after losing at home to the Auld Enemy, seemed crass and embarrassing to many. With hindsight it was useful practice.

Once in Argentina for the finals Scotland's morale was hit by press stories of boozing, gambling and womanising in the camp. Several players stayed up all night looking for it, and when it turned out to be unavailable, disappointment hit home hard.

Scottish fans struggled to erect their tents in the Argentinian heat.

MacLeod's team selection for the opening game against Peru ignored calls for prolific striker Derek Johnstone to start, despite his forty-one-goal season for Rangers, and the fact that the midfield pair of Bruce Rioch and Don Masson were so badly out of form that Derby had placed both of them on the transfer list. Masson and Rioch also upset their colleagues by eschewing the squad perm.

MacLeod didn't bother to watch Peru beforehand, expecting to roll them over easily. 'Let them worry about us!' he said, choosing to stick to the approach that had done for the likes of Dumbarton so often in the past. Veterans Teofilo Cubillas and Hector Chumpitaz didn't seem unduly worried as Peru won 3–1. Scotland were a shambles.

Subsequently winger Willie Johnston failed a random drugs test. He was found to have taken some little yellow pills which, when mixed with the sweaty palm of an official at the news conference, produced a nasty yellow stain. A bad thing, apparently.

The second game against outsiders Iran didn't provide the hoped for upturn in fortunes. It did, however, provide plenty

Dalglish passes the doping test by dribbling along a white line.

more material for the television montage sequence set to the tune of 'Don't Cry for Me Argentina', which was played again and again as the tournament progressed. Ally MacLeod with his head in his hands, Iran's comical own goal and their embarrassing equaliser, a little knot of tartan-clad supporters angrily chanting, 'We want our money back!'... Mind you, they're quite likely to chant that even when they win, so nobody took much notice.

All of which left Scotland needing to beat Holland by three clear goals. Finally Ally MacLeod was persuaded to alter the key strategy that he had employed for his international reign up to this point, which was to pick as nearly as possible the team bequeathed him by Willie Ormond.

Graeme Souness, who had brilliantly orchestrated Liverpool's European Cup triumph, was brought into midfield with Bruce Rioch, Asa Hartford and Archie Gemmill. MacLeod had stumbled – as Bobby Robson would in 1986 and 1990 – on his most potent formation as a last resort.

With their backs against the wall and an almost hopeless cause to fight for, the Scots went for it. The near certainty of failure always suits them better than the arrogant assumption of easy victory, somehow. Their familiarity with the former state of affairs probably has something to do with it.

Although Holland took the lead with a Rob Rensenbrinck penalty – a goal which meant Scotland needed four – Kenny Dalglish levelled just before half time.

Gemmill made it 2–1 with a penalty early in the second half – presumably after Joe Jordan had handled the ball – and then after sixty-eight minutes scored a goal that almost made up for all the crap that had gone before. He wriggled and jinked his way into the area, nutmegged Ruud Krol, and flicked the ball past Jongbloed into the net.

'And... Scotland are in dreamland!' went the commentary, and if they'd got another, they would have been. Never again would Archie Gemmill be described as the 'little chap who looks like Charlie Drake'. Except here, of course.

As it happens, the euphoria lasted for about three minutes, before Johnny Rep made it 3–2 and put things beyond Scotland's reach. They had the consolation of beating the eventual runners-up, and only missed out on goal difference for the second World Cup in a row. And, what do you know, in 1982 they did the same thing again.

But what if...
Scotland had got a fourth goal and knocked Holland out?

SEVENTY-ONE MINUTES. JOHNNY REP *unleashes a powerful long-range shot. It looks for all the world as though it must be a goal, until it is unexpectedly deflected over the bar by a freak air pocket created by Alan Rough's perm.*

Heartened by this stroke of luck – although MacLeod was later to claim that Rough's hair was part of a carefully devised tactical plan – Scotland lay siege to the Dutch goal. Jordan, Dalglish and Souness all go close, as does Rene van der Kerkhof at the other end, before Gemmill completes a memorable hat trick with a couple of minutes to go. Scotland are through, and as far as the tartan army are concerned, all is forgiven.

HOLLAND   1
Rensenbrinck 34 (pen)
SCOTLAND   4
Dalglish 43,
Gemmill 47 (pen), 68,
88.

Group table

	P	W	D	L	F	A	Pts
Peru	3	2	1	0	7	2	5
Scotland	3	1	1	1	6	5	3
Holland	3	1	1	1	4	4	3
Iran	3	0	1	2	2	8	1

*I*n the next phase the two top teams from each group were shuffled into two more groups of four, and the teams which topped these second-round groups would be the finalists. This seemed to FIFA the simplest way of cheating the hosts into the final itself.

Group A consisted of West Germany, Italy, Austria and Scotland, while Group B contained Argentina, Brazil, Peru and Poland.

West Germany and Italy played out a sterile goalless draw in Buenos Aires, then Scotland opened against Austria. MacLeod stuck with the side that had won him the famous victory over Holland, and the confident momentum Scotland had built up brushed aside the Austrians, 2–0, with goals from Jordan and Rioch.

They then came up against a West German team which had not impressed in Argentina so far, winning only one match – albeit a 6–0 thrashing of Mexico – and sharing goalless draws in their other three. Dieter Muller put them ahead, but Jordan's equaliser took the Scots to the top of Group A with one match to play.

The World Cup final beckoned, and a draw with Italy, who had beaten Austria only 1–0, would secure the dream. In front of a 66,000 crowd in Buenos Aires a single goal by Roberto Bettega ten minutes from time won the game. Austria's surprise 3–2 defeat of West Germany handed Scotland the unexpected bonus of a place in the third place play off.

In the final, played in Buenos Aires on 25 June, Italy would meet Argentina, who had topped Group B in controversial circumstances.

In 1976 the Argentine army had seized power in a coup, and a ruling junta of generals took control of the country. Their regime was corrupt and ruthless. As many as 11,000 so-called subversives, unwise enough to speak out against the regime, 'disappeared', to be tortured and killed.

The generals staked everything on a successful Mundial, hoping that the euphoria of becoming world champions would unite the Argentinian people, and blind them to the junta's appalling human rights record, widespread poverty, and inflation running at 600 per cent.

Argentina simply had to win the World Cup, and so, when they reached their last Group B game needing to beat Peru by at least 4–0, the generals made sure that it happened. It was alleged eight years later in the Sunday Times that Argentina's junta shipped 35,000 tons of free grain to Peru, and that the central bank of Argentina unfroze $50 million in credits for Peru. How can we get a government prepared to do that sort of thing for the national side, I wonder...?

In the game itself Peru fielded four inexperi-enced reserves, played a defender up front and missed several simple chances before Argentina opened the scoring. Peru's eccentric goalkeeper, Quiroga, was born in Argentina, and he played even more bizarrely than usual.

The final result was a 6–0 win for the home nation, and despite murmurs of discontent no concrete evidence that the match was thrown was ever uncovered. Brazil were particularly aggrieved, and their manager, Claudio Coutinho, claimed with some justification that they were the moral victors of the tournament, having special moral victors' medals struck and hiring a moral victory open-top bus.

An Italy–Argentina final in Buenos Aires would have been like a local derby. So large was the expatriate Italian community in the capital that Italy had requested that they should play their group matches there, even though this meant volunteering to share with the hosts, whom they had beaten 1–0 with a Bettega goal.

THE TEAMS

ARGENTINA
Fillol, Passarella, Olguin, L.Galvan, Tarantini, Ardiles, Gallego, Ortiz, Bertoni, Luque, Kempes.

ITALY
Zoff, Scirea, Gentile, Cuccureddu, Cabrini, Tardelli, Benetti, Antognoni, Causio, Rossi, Bettega.

rious hard man, took an early bath for looking at the referee in a funny way.

Despite these setbacks, and the award of a controversial penalty against Gaetano Scirea for pointing, Italy managed to hold on to win the 1978 World Cup, after a record-breaking twenty-eight minutes of injury time.

Caesar Luis Menotti – the Argentinian Andy Capp.

ARGENTINA	1
Kempes 70 (pen)	
ITALY	2
Rossi 29, Causio 40	

*T*he Italians, fielding nine players from the champions Juventus, were a tough and skilful side, perhaps better equipped to cope with Argentina's attacking play than the Dutch.

With the fervent torn-up-bits-of-paper-throwing support of the majority of the crowd behind them, Argentina put Italy under tremendous pressure from the start, with Kempes in particularly fine form. They could not break through, however, and the Italians scored a break-away goal through Paolo Rossi.

The shock and panic in the stadium transmitted itself to the players, and the Argentines' game fell apart. Italy went in at half-time two up, thanks to a second goal by Franco Causio.

After an unusually long interval the teams emerged with their line-ups unaltered, although the referee seemed to have grown a moustache during half-time. His attitude, too, was changed, and he had an almost military bearing.

His disciplinary style matched his gait, and he quickly gave two Italians their marching orders. Paolo Rossi was dismissed for assaulting Alberto Tarantini's fist with his front teeth and Romeo Benetti, Italy's noto-

● The aftermath of Argentina's defeat was ugly. A nation psyched up for the party of a lifetime spilled on to the streets, and rioting took place in all the cities and towns. Pizzerias and fancy Italian shoe shops were burned and looted, as the energy and enthusiasm that had gone into supporting the national team turned to resentment.

● The government was blamed for letting the people down, and the mood swung utterly against the military junta. The generals realised the game was up and went into hiding, and the left-wing guerrillas who had been quiet during the build-up to the Mundial for fear of being accused of spoiling the festivities ended their unofficial truce.

● Confusion reigned for several days. Keith Burkinshaw, the mild-mannered manager of Tottenham Hotspur, called a press conference to announce a coup. He intended to reveal that he had signed Osvaldo Ardiles and Ricardo Villa, but owing to an over-excited interpreter Burkinshaw was briefly declared President of Argentina. When he was asked how he intended to deal with the unrest in the streets, the new president's abusive outburst caused further misunderstanding, and Spurs midfielder John Pratt found himself Head of the Armed Forces with the rank of general.

● A rival faction formed behind Cesar Luis Menotti, the chain-smoking Argentine team manager, claiming that his credentials for seizing power were more impressive than Burkinshaw's FA Coaching Certificate.

● Burkinshaw tried to clear things up by announcing, through his interpreter, that he had 'captured' Ardiles and Villa. He was thrown in jail for kidnapping, and Tottenham Hotspur was declared an illegal organisation. Also detained were international observer Alf Ramsey, once of Spurs, and Graeme Souness, who never even played for the first team.
As he was led off to his cell Ramsey was heard to mutter, 'See? I told you they were animals...'

● Gradually calm returned to Argentina, and democratic elections took place later that year. The new government released papers which showed that the generals had intended to capitalise on the mood of nationalistic pride and fervour created by the Mundial by taking Argentina to war. Firstly they had planned military action to claim from Chile three contested islands in the Beagle Channel. Then, more ambitiously, the junta were looking for an opportunity to take the Falkland Islands from Great Britain. Under the new administration this attempt was never made.

● Margaret Thatcher gained a narrow victory over Michael Foot's Labour Party in the 1983 General Election. By-election defeats subsequently weakened her position, and she was unable to put into practice much of her ambitious 'Thatcherite' policies. By 1987 the mood of the country had swung against her, and Neil Kinnock was swept to power. She always maintained that if she'd had a decent war to get her teeth into she'd have been able to show people what she could do.

● Ally MacLeod returns to Scotland as their most successful manager, the only one to lead them beyond the group stages of a World Cup. He is not subdued by Scotland's 5-0 defeat by Brazil in the third place play-off, and brags that Scotland will win the European Championships and the next World Cup in Spain.

● MacLeod stands in the 1979 General Election for the SNP, and wins a seat in Parliament. His manifesto insists that any future devolved Scottish Assembly would have to be built around Don Masson and Bruce Rioch.

● An SFA spokesman admits that if Scotland had failed to beat Holland then MacLeod would have been asked to resign, and replaced by Jock Stein.

● Jock Stein, released by Glasgow Celtic, becomes manager of Leeds United in the summer of 1978. He would have walked out after fo`rty-four days to take over the Scotland reins if MacLeod had stood down, but in the event he presides over a resurgence of fortunes at Elland Road.

● Stein calmly and methodically organises a transition from the Revie era, not allowing old Revie stalwarts to dominate his team, and ruthlessly discarding them when they reach their play-by dates. In 1979 he persuades Kenny Dalglish to become the first £1 million footballer, and Leeds take the title in 1980 followed by the European Cup in 1981. Leeds, Liverpool and Everton

are closely matched throughout the early and mid-eighties.

● Ally MacLeod, having stumbled accidentally upon a winning team in Argentina, is found out as Scotland are humiliated in the qualifying tournaments for the 1980 European Championships and the 1982 World Cup, in which they were defeated home and away by Israel, who qualified in their place. At the finals Israel did Scotland proud by embarrassingly losing to group minnows New Zealand, drawing with Brazil, and beating the Soviet Union, being knocked out on goal difference.

● In 1982 Jock Stein is persuaded to take over the Scotland job.

● Despite the sustained efforts of Amnesty International, Sir Alf Ramsey was never released from jail.

● Another notable 'What if...?' moment occurred in the first round of the 1978 World Cup. In the last minute of the Group 3 match between Brazil and Sweden, English referee Clive Thomas disallowed a Brazilian goal, blowing the final whistle as Zico's corner kick was in mid-air curving into the top of the net.

It would have been a winning goal, and would have sent Brazil into second-round Group A in Austria's place.

There they could have found their way to an all-South American final against the host nation, and what an ugly affair that could have been.

Brazil's side, including the likes of Nelinho, Dirceu, Zico, Oscar, Batista and Reinaldo would have stood a good chance of beating Argentina, which would mean that many of the consequences outlined above would still be applicable.

Apart from the one about the pizzerias and fancy Italian shoe shops.

Some supporters of the sexy samba-style señors of silky South American soccer. Just like being at Elland Road, really.

If...

English players used Brazilian-style names

I **T ISN'T AS IF BRAZILIANS** don't have proper names that they could use. Look at the motor racing drivers, for example: Nelson Piquet, Emerson Fittipaldi, Rubens Barrichello and Ayrton Senna da Silva. Slightly unusual, certainly, and faintly exotic perhaps, but proper names none the less. Their footballers, however, don't feel they have arrived until they have reduced their names to a single word, the shorter the better.

You wonder whether Brazilians check Brazilian Ceefax, and assess their club's new signings by how short their names are. It might explain why Flamenco never came in for Ian Storey-Moore or Peter Rhoades-Brown.

It must be a significant rite of passage for the young Brazilian star, the moment he passes from the chorus to leading-man status. Imagine how he must feel the first time he picks up the matchday programme and finds that he is no longer Nelson Fittipaldi, say, but has become transformed for ever into something like Booto or Kicko.

I think it is greatly to the credit of our game that it accepted this convention unquestioningly, and allowed Oswaldo Giroldo to play as Juninho. It brought a glamorous sheen to every game he played – and sighs of relief from commentators such as David Pleat, who can mispronounce the name Alan Smith.

If Pelé had been a cricketer the anoraks would have painstakingly scratched him into their scorebooks as E. A. do Nascimento – not glamorous, not exciting, just foreign, somehow – but the name Pelé seems to transcend its origins and belong to the world.

Brazil's football resonates with the romance of its star monikers. Jair Ventura Filho, known as 'Jairzinho' – the suffix meaning little, to distinguish him from another earlier hero, Jair. Socrates, Rivelino, Zico, Tostão, Falcão, Mirandinha, Bebeto, Ronaldo, Romario ... Muller – after the great Gerd – and other, less notable stars named after other European greats: Tudor, Duxbury, Parlane, Hankin and Beardsmore.

But what if... the convention had caught on in Britain?

IF AN ABSURD FADDY FASHION was going to take hold anywhere it would have been Elland Road in the early seventies. Don Revie gave us dossiers, cynicism, bribery scandals. He gave us little sock tags with the players' numbers on. He had his team stand in the centre circle holding hands, and then turn round slowly in unison waving at every corner of the crowd. He changed the classic Leeds kit, which was yellow and blue, into Real Madrid's all white, in the superstitious belief that it would bring the club comparable success to the all-conquering Spanish champions. And occasionally he carried a blanket.

Then, impressed by the Brazilian displays in the Mexico World Cup of 1970, and not wanting to lose face by switching back to yellow shirts and blue shorts, he announced to a stunned British press and public that henceforth his tigerish Scottish midfielder and captain, Billy Bremner, would be known as Gingerino.

This to take effect immediately in match programmes, on the team sheets for Match of the Day, and on the player's official registration with the Football League.

Gingerino himself said, 'I think it's a very good idea, like all of the boss's ideas. Gingerino has a completely clean disciplinary record, for one thing, unlike Billy Bremner. And if it makes us play like Brazil, then I'm not complaining.'

Shortly after this, Revie – who had himself begun to answer only to the name of Gaffero – announced that other members of his multi-international squad were also to be rechristened, as these quotes, taken from seventies bubble-gum cards, will show.

GINGERINO *(Leeds United, midfield general)* *An established Scottish international, famed for his fiery temper, which he displayed during the 1974 Charity Shield match against Liverpool. A scrap led to him receiving his marching orders along with Reds star Kevinho (little Kev).*

(Far left) Billy Bremner was justly famous for his Ivy Tilsley impression. (Left) Don Revie chuckles to himself as he models the new Admiral training top.

GIRAFFEO (Leeds United, defender)
A hard-tackling centre-half with a very long neck and a little black book in which he makes notes about opposition forwards and how long their necks are. Brother of Baldo (Manchester United).

SNIFFERO (Leeds United, striker)
A slender forward with the knack of arriving just as the ball is bobbling around in the penalty area with nobody in particular looking after it. His many goals are always followed by his trademark celebration – the casual walk, one arm raised, and a smug expression that says: 'Look at me, I done it.' Shifty.

CANNONIO (Leeds United, outside-right)
Scottish international with the hardest shot in football, once timed by Norris McWhirter at quarter to eleven in the morning. Unlike Rivelino, his Brazilian counterpart, however, he has been unable to master the banana shot and can only hit the ball in straight lines. Very hard. His name does not, however, derive from this, but from his love of portly investigator, Frank Cannon.

BENCHIO (Leeds United, utility man)
Rarely, if ever, gets to start a match, but frequently called into action as a substitute. This usually only happens, however, when Leeds are at least two up, or when things are going hopelessly, irredeemably wrong. (i.e. in April and May).

● The convention catches on among the top players and, when Revie takes over the England manager's job in 1974, he insists that all members of his varied and changeable squads convert to Brazilian-style names. This leads to a minor scandal when it is revealed that Revie placed a substantial bet on the League's top scorer being someone whose name ends in a vowel.

● A particularly noteworthy player can more or less form a virtual dynasty of other professionals named in his honour. For example Benchio, as mentioned above (real name: Mick Bates), is particularly chuffed when Liverpool finds a supersub of their own in young David Fairclough and take to calling him Benchinho.

● Often a player, when making a big money move to a top club, will have it written into his contract that he is henceforth to be known by a certain title, and it begins to be commonplace for names to be registered both with the Football League and as trademarks to prevent confusion. A system similar to that operated by Equity, the Actors' Union, is devised, and there are inevitably disappointments when stars discover that many of the best hard or cool ones have gone.

● Gary Lineker, when he signs for Everton with his burgeoning England career just beginning to flourish, decides that he would like to be known as Lynx. The image of the

(Far left) Lynx (Southampton and England). (Left) Baldo's creative strand deployment never brought him his dream nickname, 'Fullheadofhairo'.

cat-like predator, hunting for scraps, particularly appeals to him, and also it sounds a bit like his real name so it will be easy to remember. Unfortunately, however, Lynx is also the name of a hideous bald alien villain on Doctor Who, and the name is consequently already registered by Southampton midfielder David Armstrong.

● Lineker is thrown at a crucial stage in the negotiations, and before he knows what has happened, his goody-two-shoes disciplinary record has earned him the trade name of Cleano. Subsequently despite years of cynical

and dirty play, and venting of foul and splenetic abuse at referees up and down the country he is unable to shake the tag, and his only consolation is that his successor as England's premier hitman, Alan Shearer, is to follow in his footsteps as Cleaninho.

● Sometimes, however, the pressure of expectation proves too much for a player tagged with a similar name to a great who has already achieved many honours in the game. No one could argue if you expressed the opinion that Baldo, England's highest goalscorer and third most-capped

Konko – he scored goals wherever he went, except Turin and Leeds.

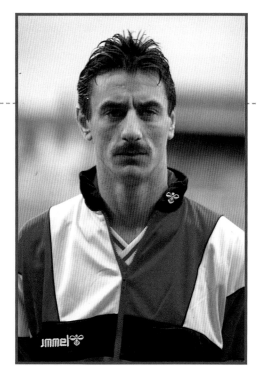

international after Mooro and 125-cap keeper Shaggo, had a marvellous career, but the same could perhaps not be said of poor Baldinho. He crumples under the weight of his huge £190,000 price tag, moving from Burnley to Spurs in 1971, and never fulfils the expectations that the well-meant tag aroused.

● *And the history of Manchester United is, of course, littered with would-be Bestinhos. Best himself was one of a select band of players talented and arrogant enough to think that their own name would suffice to generate their legend, and fortunate enough to have a suitable name for the purpose.*

● *Similarly blessed were Welshmen Gary Speed and the once lightning-fast Ian Rush. Rush, in particular, resisted great pressure to have Konko inscribed across the back of his shirt, much to the relief of John Aldridge – Rushinho, of course – and Robbie Fowler, who glories in the tag Rushinhoinho despite the widespread feeling that Konkplastero would be more appropriate.*

Shirtio – 'Call me Guvnor'.

Other current and former stars who have embraced the convention include:

SHIRTIO *(Liverpool, midfield) Former West Ham, Manchester United and Inter Milan star, who tried several times to style himself 'Guvnor', but ended up with his name as a result of an ill-judged publicity shot of him in a Manchester United shirt while still a West Ham player.*

PERMIO *(Burnley, player-manager) So tagged for his strange and crazy hair while a Newcastle player, the name stuck through a career which took him to Spurs, Marseilles, Sheffield*

Wednesday, Falkirk and Bradford City. Did investigate the possibility of using the name 'Sausages', but it had been copyrighted by the dog from That's Life!

RUDOLFO *(Manchester United, goalkeeper) The awesome Danish stopper assumed that he would be in line for an impressive name which implied hugeness or reliability, or perhaps something incorporating the idea of the Great Dane, but his team-mates registered this on his behalf before he could get round to it. Football can be a cruel game.*

LEGSNCO *(Oldham Athletic, striker) Fantastically uncoordinated and gangly forward, who began his career at Bradford City and also played for Aston Villa and Leicester City.*

PIZZAO *(Aston Villa, centre-half) Former Crystal Palace midfielder chiefly known for missing a vital penalty for England in the Euro 96 semi-final shoot-out. Earned this title when*

he trivialised this calamity by appearing in an advert for Pizza Hut with Permio and Psycho.

PSYCHO (Newcastle United, full back)
Made his reputation with fearsome displays as captain of Nottingham Forest for many years, and as an England regular. The name Psycho was much sought after, particularly, it seems, by left-backs, but this chap was the original and the best.

SIKO (West Ham, defender)
Big bullish full-back or centre-back who dearly wanted to be called Psycho, but was – unusually for him – beaten to the punch. Managed to persuade the authorities to register him as a soundalike by convincing them that he was taking the name of his hero, Bill Sikes from the film Oliver!. To perpetuate this subterfuge he took to growling 'Bullseye' out of the corner of his mouth.

DULLO (West Ham, midfield)
One-club star of the seventies and early eighties who subsequently became a television pundit. His nasal drone had the ability to send viewers to sleep by the millions.

GLENDA (Tottenham Hotspur, midfield)
Extravagantly talented creative midfielder of the eighties with ladies' hair.

COLLAPSO (Manchester United, midfield)
Long-time captain of Manchester United and England, who was prone to fall apart through injury. Highly regarded for his energy and commitment, he played ninety times for his country. His name has proved appropriate not only to his accident-prone nature but also to his off-pitch recreational activities and his management career at Middlesbrough.

CRABBO (QPR, midfield)
Much travelled midfielder, once known as 'Butch' because of a certain facial similarity to the dog from Tom and Jerry. Considering this unflattering, he adopted this name to remind everyone that he was passing the ball sideways deliberately and not because he couldn't do anything else. Also Manchester United, Chelsea, AC Milan, Paris Saint-German and Rangers.

Rushinhoinho, or Konkplastero ... the debate continues.

Psycho, the hard man and music lover, sang as he played. Here he breaks into 'Rockaway Beach' by the Ramones.

If... Smith had scored

GORDON SMITH CAN HEAR the men he now works with on the phone sometimes. 'I'm working with Gordon Smith ... yes, that one.'

Gordon Smith should have scored. He'd even scored a last-minute winning goal in a Cup final before, for Rangers in the 1978 Scottish League Cup.

Mind you, haven't we all. I know my garden frequently echoed to the sound of a familiar voice – mine – declaring:

'It's Hancock! What drama! In the dying seconds he has the chance to clinch the Cup for Stoke ... and he's done it! A shot so fierce that United keeper Paddy Roche has been carried through the net and impaled upon some railings here at Wembley.

'And dramatic news! The United directors have decided to disband the club, such is the finality and power of the goal. Chairman Edwards has just commented: "What's the point? We can never compete with a club like Stoke and their brilliant if slightly overweight striker Hancock. I've suspected it all along,

but now I may as well admit it. We are shit." '

In 1983 Gordon Smith was in a position to live the dream. Wembley. The Cup final. The last minute. Manchester United 2, Brighton and Hove Albion 2. Michael Robinson had broken away, and the beleaguered defence was drawn to him like Stan Collymore to a signing-on fee.

Robinson slipped the ball to the unmarked Smith, who steadied himself as the commentator – and very likely Gordon himself – cried: 'Smith must score!', and fired the ball at the keeper's legs. If only *Coronation Street* uniped Don Brennan had been his opponent, this tale would have had a different ending. As it was, it was blond Brad Willis lookalike Gary Bailey, and he made the save.

Inevitably United won the replay easily, and Brighton left Wembley empty-handed. Relegation to the Second Division was hardly consolation – although the prospect of Second Division football would today have Brighton fans leaping about and counting the days till next season.

Smith didn't
score.

But what if... Smith had notched?

Michael Robinson. An enigma: he lives in Spain but he's not an armed robber.

● The most profound repercussions would have fallen on Smith himself, and not all of them that welcome. The close proximity of Michael Robinson, a strapping lad of no fixed hairstyle, would almost certainly have meant that Smith was in line for a lingering and passionate congratulatory kiss from the Eire international, and it is this prospect which many experts believe may have caused Smith's fateful hesitation.

● Brighton would have held on to Gary Stevens (a good thing) and Steve Foster (a good thing for Luton Town), whose Brian May hairstyle is coveted by Manager Jimmy Melia.

● The European Cup Winners' Cup campaign would have been a brief flirtation – à la Robbie Williams and Anna Friel – with the Seagulls crashing out 4–0 on aggregate to Hungarian cable TV operators Videoton.

● United sack Ron Atkinson for his lack of success, and for his tactlessness in wearing more silverware at Wembley than the club has picked up in recent years.

● Candidates to replace Big Ron include ordinary-sized Ron Saunders, John Toshack and Graham Taylor, the manager with the Midas touch at Lincoln and Watford.

Big Ron Atkinson played football for fun.

● Taylor gets the job, and clears out Bailey, Muhren, Wilkins and Coppell, and, after a surprise auditor's report, Nobby Stiles, who United had mistakenly kept under contract since 1974. By keeping very quiet and hiding behind a boiler, Nobby had, without kicking a ball, been drawing a wage of thirteen guineas a week.

● At Brighton, Jimmy Melia, the man who'd managed them to Cup triumph, is also sacked for supposed 'financial irregularities'. Apparently, the substantial cash rewards the Cup had brought had gone missing, and investigations revealed that Melia had blown it all on a series of dubious hair restoration and transplant schemes, which left Brighton in dire straits but Jimmy looking like Michael Bolton.

● Graham Taylor puts silverware on the United mantelpiece within three years, and many of that Third Division championship-winning side are still held in much affection by the supporters of Manchester City.

● Nick Hancock's mould-breaking unfunny bloopers video, *And Smith Did Score*, is a best-seller in the Brighton area, where Gordon Smith has become the town's very popular mayor.

Steve Foster's famous Captain's headband.

If... I had been William Webb Ellis's games teacher

(L-R) William, Webb, Ellis.

IN THE AUTUMN OF 1823 William Webb Ellis, a Manchester-born pupil at Rugby School, was playing football. Not football as we know it today, exactly, because outfield players were allowed to handle the ball as long as they didn't run with it, and there was a much more relaxed attitude towards kicking and punching members of the other team.

At some point in the match, Webb Ellis – displaying the arrogance that comes free with a second surname – unaccountably decided to flout what was pretty much the only actual rule in football in those days, and ran with the ball in his hands through the bemused ranks of the opposition and scored a goal.

His PE teacher, exhibiting a liberalism far from common in members of that calling, said, 'Well done, Webb Ellis, you've invented rugby! Any chance of tickets for the international?' And the lad was carried shoulder-high by his team-mates to the changing rooms where he showed them how to light their own farts and get into university without being able to read or write.

Rugby School, where boys prayed daily to be allowed to play football again.

But what if... young William had had a normal PE teacher, and not one whose break-time tea had clearly been spiked with opium?

*I*ACTUALLY TRAINED as a games teacher, and there is a proper procedure for dealing with incidents of this kind. A short but confident blow on the whistle is recommended, followed by a weary shout of, 'Webb Ellis? Here! Now!'

You would then take the ball from the boy, roll it around in a muddy puddle, throw it in his face and say, 'Right, now go to the changing rooms and clear all the pubic hair out of the shower plugholes. And be quick about it!' (Remember to emphasise your enjoyment in inflicting this punishment, because spite is the games master's friend.)

Actually, in 1823 attitudes to school discipline were apparently even tougher, and Webb Ellis's behaviour should strictly speaking have landed him on a fast clipper to Trinidad and/or Tobago, working below decks among the rats and demented, scurvy-ridden, sex-starved sailors until he learned to respect his elders and betters. And PE teachers.

It beggars belief that William Webb Ellis's little bit of mischief could have spawned two separate new sports which are now played around the world – arguably three, if you count the horrible helmeted pantomime that

they play in the USA. Imagine if the football authorities now, eager for rule changes to revitalise the game, asked a bunch of schoolboys for their suggestions, and announced the following innovations, with immediate effect at all levels:

1. Spuds in. The ancient selection process of 'one potato, two potato' could effectively dismantle the two-tier Premiership created by spiralling transfer fees. You can have as many Sir John Halls as you like, but a quick round of spuds before each game leaves you with Brian Deane while Sheffield United end up with Alan Shearer.

2. Last one picked goes in goal. Developments in keeper coaching have made scoring more difficult, but under kickabout rules you're not allowed in goal unless you are (a) another player's kid brother, or (b) crap. QED: more goals.

3. Only headers, volleys and dead good goals count. A qualitative masterstroke, ridding the game of vulgar tap-ins, own goals and toe pokes, thereby forcing

coaches to concentrate on technique rather than fitness.

4. *Your mum's shouting. Not strictly speaking a rule, but a guideline which keeps players under their mums' authority during a game. Good for discipline and an attractive alternative to players' agents.*

5. *No kick-offs, no half-time, no offsides. Fripperies, irrelevancies and affectations all. Other non-essentials to go include crossbars, referees, managers and pitch dimensions.*

6. *Next goal wins. Provides a result and gives hope to any team 4–0 down with a minute to go. Now the consolation goal can be the winner.*

Getting a Ball: boys had to carefully eat a live pig, leaving only the bladder.

Q. P .R. Williams (QPR and Wales).

My theory is that William Webb Ellis had something on the headmaster. The absurd degree to which he was indulged during his years at Rugby can be seen by looking at the results from School Sports Day in his last year:

100m – Winner: W Webb Ellis (using horse)
Steeplechase – Winner: W Webb Ellis (using horse)
400m – Winner: W Webb Ellis (using horse)
High Jump – Winner: W Webb Ellis (using house)
Jumping over Mini Minor – Winner: D. McKenzie

Still, that's a public school education for you. If Webb Ellis had been at St Mary's in the Cray Secondary Modern would Will Carling have been captain of England's St Mary's in the Cray Secondary Modern team?

No, if I had been William Webb Ellis's games teacher, there would now be no such thing as rugby, union or league, and:

● Lots of sportsmen who currently play rugby would have gone into football. There would be plenty more big shithouse defenders sprinkled throughout the game, and others would have made a limited success of the different code.

● Rob Andrew proves a fast and fit forward, and his propensity for booting the ball over the bar makes him the natural replacement for Lee Chapman at Arsenal in the eighties.

● Jeremy Guscott spends twelve years of his fourteen-year career injured, but still manages to make a packet out of lucrative modelling contracts and spin-offs. Like Jamie Redknapp.

● Billy Beaumont, Gareth Chilcott and Brian Moore remain at non-league level, but Robin Cousins proves a popular team captain on *Question of Sport*,

enjoying a strange camp rapport with Ian Botham, and pantomimes in the West Country are considerably less frighteningfor the small children they are meant to entertain.

● Wales, featuring J. P. R. Williams, Gareth Edwards and Barry John, qualify for the World Cups of 1974 and 1978. Williams becomes the darling of Loftus Road when, after ten years with his only club, he changes his name to Quentin so that he can be Q. P. R. Williams.

● Western Samoa have an alarmingly fast and strong football team, which reaches the semi-final of the 1994 World Cup.

● Australia and New Zealand decline to enter, their whole attention taken by their national sport of sheep-shearing. That's right, shearing.

● Hare-coursing is the jewel in BBC Sport's crown, and the top sport at Oxford and Cambridge universities.

● Twickenham is a quiet, chic suburb of London, unmolested by champagne-swilling, arse-baring, jeep-driving, braying posh goons who wear those oily coats with the corduroy collars.

● Erika Roe wanders the streets, lost, forlorn, a woman without purpose.

Gareth Edwards
(Swansea City
and Wales) –
sent off forty-
two times in
his career for
hand ball.

1966
And All That

A SHORT STORY BY CHRIS ENGLAND

WEMBLEY 1966. The dazzling sunlight. The Kenneth Wolstenhome commentary. The people on the pitch. The bright red shirts. Nobby Stiles dancing around with the little gold trophy on his head. Bobby Moore trying to maintain his dignity perched on his teammates' shoulders, careful to compose a proper smile, knowing that the pictures being taken would be reproduced over and over.

Take that away and what have we got left? What else can we crow about as a nation? We'd have to hark back to the Second World War for the last time we beat the Germans when it mattered – although Heaven knows we do enough of that, too.

Part of the magic and mythology surrounding the victory lies in the fact that the match itself featured a classic 'What if ...' moment, when Geoff Hurst's shot cannoned down off the crossbar and on to, over, or alongside the goal line. What if the Russian linesman had the benefit of stop-frame video equipment before making his decision? Or better still,

what if he'd had the Israeli virtual reality missile tracking technology used by Andy Gray to determine, 31 years later, that the goal should never have stood? What if Roger Hunt had chased the loose ball and tucked it away instead of wheeling away, arms in the air, hoping a goal would be given?

And if the goal had been disallowed, would the Germans then have got a second wind and surged to victory? Would Jimmy Greaves have forgotten himself and skipped, David Pleat-style, ecstatically across the Wembley turf, before suddenly remembering that he was supposed to be disappointed? Or would England, the stronger side in extra time, have won anyway, leaving Scottish pundits to moan that there wasn't enough injury time, or the German shirts were too difficult to see ...?

It was all a long time ago and so we have treated this 'What if...' in a different way, with a short story set both in the present day and in the aftermath of that sunny afternoon in the summer of '66.

ENGLAND 3 GERMANY W. 2

NEIL PETTINGER clutched his new treasures to his chest as he trotted up the steps leading to the street from Sloane Square tube station. Straight away he spotted his bus, the 137 to Streatham, swinging round the corner, and he broke into a shuffly little run to catch it. He made it just in time, and half-scrambled half-fell into a seat as the bus pulled away. But an elderly man who had been on the same tube train as Neil was not so lucky, and he quickly turned to hail a cab.

Neil sat with his carrier bag on his lap and congratulated himself on a morning well spent. He had been to a football book, programme and memorabilia fair at Earl's Court called 'Soccerabilia', and allowed himself a smirk at the thought of all the nerds wandering around there in their anoraks with their thick spectacles stuck together with bits of Sellotape.

'Poor sad goofs!' he thought to himself. They should go to that place next door to Safeway where Neil got his own thick spectacles, plus a free pair of prescription sunglasses. He still had the special offer leaflet in his anorak pocket.

Once he had been like those sad get-a-lifes, he thought, but now he was a professional. A few years ago his collection of football reference books had become so comprehensive, and his letters castigating broadcasters and journalists for minor statistical and factual errors had become so insistent, that he began to get calls at all times of the day and night asking for

information which it seemed only he was in a position to provide. The trickle became a flood, and he hit upon the notion of charging a small finders' fee, using a finicky little invoicing system of his own devising.

Happy is the man who can make a living at his hobby. Neil was eventually able to pack in his job at the wooden box factory and become a full-time statistician and football expert. He had even, once or twice, been the man who counted goal attempts for Sky TV, and the following night was due to work on an FA Cup third round tie at Loftus Road.

The old Routemaster bus trundled into Battersea and stopped. An old lady with a wicker shopping basket on wheels barked it down Neil's shin as he moved over to let her sit down. He bit his tongue and glared out of the window at no one in particular. If he had looked behind him he might have seen a neat-looking gentleman, around sixty, hurriedly paying off a cab, then jogging after the bus and leaping nimbly on to the back step. But he didn't, so he didn't.

Once back at his flat Neil tipped a can of baked beans into a pan on the stove and stuck a couple of slices of bread in the toaster, before laying his purchases out on the kitchen table for inspection.

He was particularly pleased with a delightfully obscure complete history of Austrian soccer to 1973, and a first edition of Derek Dougan's novel *The Footballer* from 1974 which he hoped would rank alongside the Jackie Groves books of

Jimmy Greaves. Then, of course, there was the box, which he had only obtained after a slightly strange and vaguely unpleasant incident.

The box itself wasn't at all strange. Cardboard, a foot square, with some German writing on it, it contained a couple of dozen spools of elderly Super 8 film. As he turned them over in his hands, Neil saw that each was labelled with a date and a football match, such as 'Schalke 04 v IFC Nürnberg, Nov. 1965', or 'B. Dortmund v Schalke 04, Feb. 1966'.

'Ah, the mighty blue-and-whites,' muttered Neil to himself. 'Schalke 04, the lions of Gelsenkirchen, the powerhouse of the Ruhr ... he must have been a fan.'

Meaning not only the presumably amateur film-maker, but also the elderly gentleman who had so animatedly tried to persuade him to part with his purchase. Neil had just handed over fifteen pounds for the box to the stallholder when this bloke had barged up.

'Fifteen?' he had gasped breathlessly. 'I'll give you twenty!'

The stallholder's fingers had tightened on the box momentarily, but then he let Neil take it. 'I'm sorry, sir ...' he started to say.

'Thirty!' cried the stranger.

'I'm very sorry,' said the stallholder, and Neil could see he really was, 'but I've already sold it to this gentleman for ...' – and his lips tightened into a snarl – ' ... fifteen quid.'

Neil had turned and walked towards the exit, and the man had followed, desperately upping his offers in an urgent Scots accent. 'Sixty ... seventy-five pounds. Come on, son, I'll give ye seventy-five for it. What do ye say?'

The more the man offered, however, the more determined Neil became to hang on to the box. 'It's not for sale,' he said, firmly. 'Sorry ...'

NEIL FINISHED his beans on toast and stuck the plate into the sink, where, if things ran to form, it would stay for at least the next forty-eight hours. He picked up the box of spools and went through to the library.

On the original designs for the small flats in Neil's block the room would certainly have been a living room, or possibly a diner-loungette, but Neil put shelves on all the walls from floor to ceiling, and since he only ever dealt with enquiries by phone he felt justified in describing it as a library. It gave him authority, he felt, and he charged extra accordingly.

As well as the hundreds of reference books and video cassettes he had accumulated, Neil already had several dozen reels of amateur football films. He especially liked to see film of players and games from the sixties, the fifties, and even earlier, that television only had in black and white – if at all. He liked the strange, slightly unreal quality of the colours in the old home movies, and the sense of the cameraman having actually gone to the game as a punter.

He set up his projector, closed the curtains, and waggled his fingers over the box deciding where to start. Here was one in an old envelope. Neil took it out. There was no label on it. He tutted, then grinned. A challenge. Excellent.

The film whirred into the projector, and Neil reached for a German football almanac, ready to identify Schalke 04's opponents of thirty years earlier. Hang on, though ... Surely this ground was Wembley ...?

Red and white figures danced in and out of focus, familiar passages of play purred by from unfamiliar angles, and Neil quickly realised he was watching the World Cup final of 1966.

'Phew! The lucky sod!' he whistled. 'How did he get there? He's practically on the goal line ...' The screen momentarily filled with black as Hans Tilkowski backed up practically on top of the camera before launching a goal kick away into the far distance.

A flicker, and then Hurst was wheeling away in triumph. Obviously Moore's quick free kick had caught out not only the German defence but also the amateur film-maker. A little later and the ball was loose in the goalmouth only a few feet away from the lens. Banks dived across, Weber stuck out a boot, and the ball hit the net. Crazy kaleidoscope patterns filled the screen, and as they gradually calmed down Neil could see that his German friend had carried on filming while jumping up and down with his arms in the air.

A shot of the players sitting, standing around, drinking, preparing for extra time, and then it was upon him and past almost before he recognised it. Alan Ball sprinting down the wing, the cross whipped in, Geoff Hurst controlling the ball, turning, shooting, the ball cannoning down off the crossbar and out, Roger Hunt turning away to claim the goal, Bobby Charlton not really looking as though he thinks it will be given, the referee talking to the linesman, waving, pointing. Flukily, miraculously, the German film-maker had captured it all from only feet away.

Neil's mind and his pulse raced as he wound the film back to watch it again. The most disputed goal in football history, filmed from the perfect angle, and he had the film. He must be able to tell, must be, if the ball was over the line or not.

The second time he was ready for it. The ball smashing into the crossbar and down, and ... God! It wasn't over! The whole of the ball ... it had to be the whole of the ... Watch it again.

Hurst thumped the ball against the bar again, and this time Neil wasn't so certain. If only he could hold on that frame, but he wasn't sure that his projector could do that without setting fire to the film. Then he had a brainwave – get it transferred to video.

Last Christmas he'd taken his mother's home movies to be converted on to cassette, and that had worked all right apart from the gratuitous plinky-plonk music that the man in the shop had added on, which had the effect of making even the most mundane of family occasions feel like a Harold Lloyd comedy. Neil's mother had been especially perplexed at the use of 'The Entertainer' to accompany shots of Neil's father's funeral.

'It wouldn't have been so bad if he'd been remotely entertaining when he was alive,' she'd said, 'but he wasn't.'

Neil quickly spooled the precious World Cup film on to the reel, grabbed his anorak, and ran out of the flat. When he reached the street he headed left towards the camera shop. In the café over the road a white-haired gentleman watched him go, then finished his cup of coffee and got to his feet.

AN HOUR LATER NEIL arrived home. He had already begun to formulate a feverish plan to write a book based on the film. He'd find out who the film-maker was, and why he'd kept quiet all these years. It might make a nice little volume, and he could maybe do a television documentary as well, which would be a great little calling-card when he tried for more work at Sky.

He let himself back into his flat and made for the kettle. A glance into his library stopped him in his tracks, however, and his mouth dropped open in horror. The room had been ransacked. Books had been taken from the shelves and strewn around the floor, video tapes pulled from their boxes, and the Super 8 films were all unspooled in a sprawling spaghetti pile in the middle of the floor.

Neil blinked at the shambles that had been made of his various filing systems and collections, and shuffled slowly into the room. It was impossible to tell if anything was missing, or if he was merely the victim of senseless vandalism.

'Shit!' he said, as he recovered a little composure. 'Shit fuck bugger bloody arse.'

'Stand very still,' said a voice from behind him, its unexpectedness calculated to make standing very still more than usually difficult at that precise moment. Neil jumped a foot into the air, and only stood very still once he had landed. He felt something cold and hard pressed into the back of his neck, and a practised hand rifling through his anorak pockets.

'All right, turn round, very slowly.'

Neil did as he was told, and came face to face with the elderly man from the programme fair, and a large and efficient-looking pistol.

'Where is it?' rasped the Scotsman.

'At the end of the corridor on the left,' blurted Neil, so anxious to help the man with the gun that the absurdity of the notion that a man might follow him home, ransack his flat and hold him up at gunpoint just to ask him where his toilet was didn't occur to him until too late.

'Don't play silly buggers with me, lad. I know how to use this, you know.'

'I wouldn't exactly need an instruction manual myself,' thought Neil.

'I found this,' said the Scotsman, holding up the envelope that the World Cup film had been in. 'Where's the film that was inside it?'

Neil was alarmed. The moment he'd laid eyes on the big gun, he'd decided to give this man whatever he wanted, and now it turned out he couldn't.

'I haven't got it,' Neil said, starting to panic. 'I can get it for you, but not until tomorrow.' He explained about getting it converted to video. The man looked suddenly tired.

'Oh well,' the Scotsman said, more or less to himself. 'I've waited thirty years. Another day won't hurt.' He slumped into an armchair, and the gun dangled loose in his hand. The air of menace that had hung about him was gone.

Neil was confused. A moment ago he had feared for his life, but now his assailant looked rather forlorn.'Would ... would you like a cup of tea?' Neil ventured. 'I was just going to have one before you ... well, before you stuck a gun in my neck.'

'Aye, thanks, lad. I'm sorry about the ... well ...' and the Scotsman tucked the gun inside his coat. 'Force of habit, I'm afraid.'

Neil put the kettle on, and wondered what the hell was going on. The squeal of a chair leg on the lino made him jump, and he realised his visitor had joined him in the kitchen.

'I owe ye an explanation, son. The name's Dalgety. Jim Dalgety.'

'Ding dingading ding ...' thought Neil, to the tune of the James Bond theme – and he wasn't far wrong.

TWENTY-NINE YEARS before, in early August 1966, Jim Dalgety was having the worst week of his life. He had pinned all his hopes on the West Germans to humiliate the bloody English, having been bitterly betrayed by the French, the Mexicans, the Uruguayans, the Argentines, and the Portuguese. Now he had to endure the triumphant cackling of the bloody English in his office, and they were all bloody English except for him. What made it worse was that they were posh English, public school English most of them, who didn't share his own deep passion for football but had adopted the game for the summer because the bloody English were winning. Ordinarily, of course, rugby union, golf and cricket were the sports of the British Secret Service.

To cheer himself up, Jim went to the Odeon to see *Goldfinger*. In the film Britain's top secret agent was a Scotsman and drove a modified silver Aston Martin with a bullet-proof metal shield that pinged up behind the back window and rocket launchers which poked out of little hatches by the headlights. He got off with a number of gorgeous women, played golf with a megalomaniac supervillain, bowler hat Frisbee with an oriental thug, and saved Fort Knox from a nuclear explosion. Jim enjoyed the film, but knew that the real life of a Scottish secret agent was slightly different. He made his way back to the office – and the pile of dockets and chits he was filing – in his unreliable green Morris Traveller, which he believed to be possibly the only car in London with woodworm.

He winced as he entered the open-plan office and saw Charles Vermont Sellotaping a newspaper photograph of Geoff Hurst to the wall of his cubicle.

VERMONT WAS in his mid-thirties, and had the aloof assurance that was the hallmark of a top-class public school education. He had been riding Dalgety remorselessly more or less ever since the final whistle of the World Cup final.

'Thought you might like to see what a real footballer looks like, Jock,' he sneered.

'Aye, and perhaps you'd like to see what a real smack in the gob looks like, you big girl,' Jim growled, squaring up to his tormentor.

Vermont peered down his nose. 'Now, now. Assaulting me might make you feel better, Jock, but after you'd been thrown out of here on your ear you'd be broke and unemployed and we'd still be *World Champions!*'

The last two words were bellowed in Jim's face to cheers from the other occupants of the office, and Vermont pivoted quickly out of Jim's reach and sat down, leaving him clenching his fists and burning with anger and frustration in the middle of the room as Strowger, the supervisor, strode in.

'What's the matter with you, Dalgety? You look constipated. No work to do? Come with me. Vermont? You too.' And he strode out again.

A hush fell over the crowded office, and the banter of a few moments ago was forgotten. The agents only ever saw Strowger when there was a field mission in the offing, and they watched Dalgety and Vermont with envy as the chosen men straightened their ties and trotted after the supervisor.

Strowger was waiting for them in his private office, and he got straight down to business.

'Now then, Dalgety. You've got a bit of German, haven't you?'

'Ein smattering, sir,' Dalgety smirked, affecting a little Connery-esque drollery.

'Ah yes, don't tell me,' said Strowger, frowning. 'That's railway station, isn't it?'

Dalgety thought about explaining his feeble joke, and then thought better of it.

Strowger peered down his nose at Dalgety's file, which was open on the desk in front of him, and continued: 'I understand you took a bullet in the leg going over the Wall last year? Good show ... Good show ...'

'Thank you, sir,' said Dalgety, neglecting to mention that on the occasion in question his own gun had gone off in his back pocket and shot him in the arse.

Strowger leaned over the desk and looked him straight in the eye. 'Got a job for you,' he said, 'in Germany. West Germany this time, so there won't be any shenanigans with snipers or sentry posts. Not unless you get very unlucky indeed, or lost. Vermont here will be your handler. There's

an item we need retrieving from a gentleman called Heisenmatt in Koblenz. Trouble is, he probably won't want to give it to you. Now you could just steal it, of course, but we also need to know if there is a copy, so your mission will be to get close to this Heisenmatt, and gain his confidence. Think you can do it?'

'Of course, sir.'

'Good show ... Good show. Well, see Section Nine for your travel bumph and your fake ID, and you can read the briefing on the way. Vermont? You'll report daily on the secure line. Clear?'

'Right, sir.'

Dalgety and Vermont stood, and paused a moment, unsure whether or not they had been dismissed. Strowger hunched over another file for a moment, then he got to his feet, still reading, and wandered over to a door which the agents knew led to an executive washroom. They took this as their cue to leave, and as the door closed behind them they each clearly heard the supervisor breaking wind. Each of them thought of a different joke about making a daily report, but the hostility between them was such that each kept it to himself.

As Dalgety and Vermont collected their documentation from Section Nine in the basement of the building the Englishman offered an olive branch. 'It'll be nice to work with you on a case, Jim,' he said.

'Um ... thanks, Vermont,' Dalgety growled.

'It'll give me the chance to talk you through the World Cup final a few more times, at any rate.'

The Scotsman snarled.

EARLY NEXT MORNING a bleary Jim Dalgety boarded the crowded Harwich boat-train at Liverpool Street station and stumbled the length of the train forwards and backwards before he found his partner. Vermont had managed to keep a whole compartment to himself by pulling down the blinds and jamming the door shut with his briefcase. He looked up from a silver service breakfast tray as Dalgety succeeded in wrenching the sliding door open where other, more timid, passengers had failed.

'Morning. Good trick, that, isn't it? Fancy a kipper?'

Dalgety grunted, and accepted a cup of coffee. After half an hour or so he felt a little more human, and took a look at the file he had been given. A blood-red stamp in the top corner said 'For Your Eyes Only'.

'Huh! Look at that!' he snorted, pointing it out to Vermont, who peered over, then shrieked.

'Oh! Don't show me that, you idiot! Can't you see what it says? "For Your Eyes Only"?'

'Yeah, but that means what's inside. Surely you're allowed to see the stamp saying "For Your Eyes Only"?'

'Absolutely not,' Vermont insisted primly.

'Well, in that case I'll have to kill you, then, won't I?'

muttered Dalgety with unpleasant relish, and conversation stopped.

The two men travelled over to the Hook of Holland on the ferry, a journey which Dalgety enlivened by drinking the entire contents of a gift pack of little bottles of whisky while watching Vermont trying to get the cafeteria to provide a pot of tea rather than a plastic mug with a teabag floating in it.

Then they continued by train, following the course of the Rhine upstream towards the Alps.

The black spires of the war-scarred Kölner Dom were silhouetted against an orange evening sky before either of them mentioned their mission.

'How long to Koblenz?' Dalgety asked.

'Less than an hour now, I should think,' replied Vermont.

'Perhaps we should discuss what we're going to do when we get there.'

'I thought a spot of dinner, if we can find a tolerable restaurant. Of course, German cuisine isn't exactly the world's finest. Mostly boiled cabbage and boiled sausages. They will boil things, your Germans.

'Mind you, rather that than God knows what stuffed into a sheep's stomach as your national dish, eh Jim?'

Dalgety was too tired to rise to that particular bait. 'I meant the case, the mission, you know ...' he said, wafting a hand at the file.

'Righto, OK. It seems that this fellow Heisenmatt owns a small photographic shop in the old part of Koblenz. Your cover is that you are a holidaymaker ...'

'Oh yes,' said Dalgety, 'and my cover identity is a Mr James Dalgetybridge. I mean, what sort of an ID is that, eh?'

'Section Nine know what they are doing,' said Vermont.

'What's yours?'

'I am using the name Charles Vermontstone, since you ask.'

Dalgety snorted scornfully, and Vermont continued. 'Listen, you are a holidaymaker, OK, and you have a home movie camera that needs fixing.'

'So I go into Heisenmatt's shop and say, "Can you fix this?", and he says, "Certainly, sir. Ready Thursday." Then what?'

'The rest is up to you. He is a home movie enthusiast. It should be possible to strike up some kind of rapport.'

'Terrific. And the item? The item we are supposed to be retrieving? Presumably it's photographs, or a film, is it?'

Vermont pursed his lips. 'I can't tell you that, yet, Jim. That information is on a "need to know" basis.'

'I'm going to need to know sooner or later, aren't I? Or else how do I know what I'm after?'

'When the time comes you will be told,' said Vermont, pompously, trusting that when the time came he himself would be told.

'Yeah, it's got to be photographs,' said Dalgety, knowing that speculation would irritate his companion. 'And I imagine Heisenmatt is trying to blackmail one of our elders and betters. Still, it won't be the first time I've risked my neck in the National Interest, only to find I'm really doing a little favour for one of Strowger's mates.'

Vermont said nothing, and Dalgety got up and went for a cigarette in the corridor.

THE TRAIN PULLED into Koblenz station at 7.04, two minutes early. 'Coh! I thought the trains were meant to run on time here ...' trilled Vermont as he stepped on to the platform.

They walked into the town and booked themselves into a small hotel using the names Dalgetybridge and Vermontstone. When he got up to his room Dalgety slung his case on to the bed and had a wash, scrubbing the long journey from his face and hair. Changing his shirt, he glanced out of the window and saw that he had rather a splendid view.

The town of Koblenz was built at the confluence of the Mosel and the Rhine. A large open Platz with seats and promenades had been created at the point where the two mighty rivers met, so that people could stand, sit, talk and walk as they indulged the human fascination with watching water moving. It was this Platz, and the rivers beyond, that Dalgety's window looked out on.

As he admired the view he caught sight of Vermont strolling away from the hotel towards the promontory, and he remembered that he had agreed to dine with the irritating Englishman.

Vermont was leaning on a railing gazing out over the water as Dalgety joined him.

'It's like standing on the bow of a great ship, don't you think, Jim?'

'Not really.'

'Oh, come on. There's no poetry in your soul, that's your trouble.'

'It's not that. It's just that the water's going the wrong way, isn't it?'

The Mosel, to their left, and the Rhine, to their right, were indeed joining and flowing away from them to the North. Vermont blinked as he took this obvious point in.

'It's like standing on the stern of a great ship, don't you think, Jim?' he said, eventually.

'Oh come on. I thought we were going to eat.'

A few minutes later the two agents sat in a small restaurant off the main square. Vermont was having an animated discussion with the waiter.

'Anyway,' he was saying, 'the ball was definitely over the line.'

'Nein, nein, nein ...' the waiter insisted, trying to demonstrate with cutlery and a bread roll.

'The linesman said it was over, and he was the best placed to see, now wasn't he?'

'Ah, but it was not fair play. The linesman was Russian. They hate us Germans,' the waiter argued.

'Well, I should have thought the fact that you killed twenty million of them in the war might explain that, what do you think?' Vermont sneered smugly, and the waiter turned on his heel and disappeared into the kitchen.

'That told him, eh, Jim?' Vermont smirked. 'One–nil to me, I think.'

Dalgety gazed gloomily out of the window, and when an hour and forty five minutes had elapsed without any sign of any food arriving he got up, leaving Vermont alone in the restaurant.

THE FOLLOWING MORNING Dalgety walked out of the hotel and across the square. He lit a cigarette and leaned on the railings, watching a couple of big black low-slung barges oozing slowly along the Rhine.

He had chosen to wear his own clothes – plain white shirt, dark suit and tie – rather than Section Nine's parody holiday-maker package of flowery shirt, big shorts, and sandals. He had explained to Vermont that this was because his practice when undercover was to keep artifice to a minimum, but really it was because he didn't want to look like a halfwit. He glanced towards the hotel, and saw Vermont strolling in his direction.

'Morning, Jim,' the Englishman called. 'Fags for breakfast again?'

'Hallo, Vermont,' Dalgety grunted, and turned back to face the rivers.

'OK, today is M One.' Dalgety frowned, and Vermont elucidated. 'That's what I'm calling it in the report. M for mission, one for Day One. See?'

'I see.'

'Now then. Here's the cine camera.'

Vermont handed Dalgety a grey cuboid box with an eye-piece at one end and a lens at the other.

'You wander about taking some film of the town this morning, and I'm reliably informed by Section Nine that it will pack in after a minute or two. A cog will fall off, or something, apparently. Then you toddle off to Heisenmatt's shop and ask him to fix it, and take it from there. Roger?'

'Absolutely.'

'Rendezvous here at 1800 hours for a full report. OK?'

'What are you doing all day?'

'Oh, apparently there's a rather splendid golf course not far away, so don't you worry about me, Jim.'

'Hang on,' Dalgety growled, 'I could be done in half an hour. I wouldn't mind a round myself.'

'Oh no, Jim, you need all your concentration and energy for the job in hand. Good luck!'

Vermont trotted off to the hotel, and Dalgety watched for a moment, then turned and spat disgustedly into the river below.

'It's just a bloody holiday for him, this ...' he muttered to himself.

THE ELDERLY JIM DALGETY paused at this point in his story, and got up to make more tea. Neil Pettinger had warmed to the old chap, but still didn't feel like passing any comment of the sarcastic 'make yourself at home' variety. He looked at the envelope which the World Cup film had been in. Dalgety had been turning it round in his hands as he spoke, and it now lay on the kitchen table. Neil could read the address, and the name which had meant nothing to him before now rang a bell.

'Wolfgang Heisenmatt, Koblenz,' he read to himself. 'The camera shop man. Well, well, well ...'

Dalgety plonked two mugs of tea down on the table, and sat down again.

HEISENMATT'S SHOP was a rather poky establishment on one of the narrow cobbled streets leading from the main square in the heart of the old town. As Jim Dalgety entered a little tingly bell summoned the proprietor from a back room. Although the building was old, the shop's interior was modern, decorated with bright neon advertisements for Kodak film and a cardboard cutout of a girl in a bikini using a snapshot camera without even looking through the viewfinder.

A shortish man in his late thirties emerged from the back of the shop and raised his eyebrows inquisitively at Dalgety.

'Excuse me, I'd like to speak to Herr Heisenmatt,' Dalgety said, in German.

'I am Heisenmatt,' said the man.

'Ah, good morning. I have a problem with my cine camera, and I was told at my hotel that you were the man to see.'

Heisenmatt seemed pleased, but took the camera from Dalgety without a word. Dalgety sighed inwardly, as the man did not seem naturally chatty and thus easy to form a spurious rapport with.

After turning the camera upside down, and rattling it, Heisenmatt asked: 'There is a film inside?'

'Yes.'

'Important?'

'Well, it is just shots of Koblenz. I am a holidaymaker.' Jim felt he should establish his false identity right from the start.

'I must open it up. I will try not to damage your film, but it is impossible to be certain.'

'I understand,' Jim said.

'Return this afternoon,' Heisenmatt said, and disappeared into the back room again.

Jim lingered a moment or two to be sure that the man wasn't going to return, and then walked out into the street. It was clear that he had not been outstandingly successful in his first encounter with Wolfgang Heisenmatt.

'Bugger it all,' he thought, and went into the first bar he saw for a drink.

As he sipped a lager Dalgety wondered how he could

possibly strike up a friendship, or even a conversation, with the miserable shopkeeper. He would return to check if the little German had managed to fix Section Nine's cine camera, but then what? Ask him out? It seemed hopeless.

Another customer rustled a newspaper, trying to fold it with the sports page uppermost. Dalgety glanced across, and saw that it was Heisenmatt. He'd obviously come into the bar for his lunch, for there was a beer and a sandwich on the table in front of him. Although Heisenmatt looked as if he wanted to be alone with his paper and lunch. Dalgety knew this was a heaven-sent opportunity.

'Mind if I join you?' he asked, in German, sidling into a chair opposite the German shopkeeper. Heisenmatt recognised him and grunted a surly acknowledgement before returning to his reading.

'You are reading about football, I see ...' Dalgety began.

'That's right, and what makes you think I wish to discuss football with you, Englishman?' Heisenmatt snapped, with surprising venom. Dalgety was rather taken aback.

'Well, for a start, I'm not ...' he stuttered.

'What do you know of football, with your so-called "fair play" and your "this is not cricket"?' Heisenmatt went on. 'You, you who have stolen the World Cup from us with your lying, cheating behaviour!'

'My dear Herr Heisenmatt ...'

'I am not your dear Mister Englishman. In the shop I will be polite but here I am having my lunch, and I do not wish to sit with so-called "sporting" chaps who will claim a goal that has bounced out a foot from the goal line. I myself saw it, Englishman! I was there!'

Dalgety could contain himself no longer. The frustration of the past week, the bitter gall of England's win, and now to be taken for an Englishman! It was too much.

'If you call me Englishman one more time so help me I'll tear your head off and spit in your neck!' he roared. 'I'm a Scotsman, do ye hear me? A Scotsman, from Bonnie Scotland, and if you think I take so much as one tiny ounce of pleasure from the World Cup you're sorely mistaken!'

The hum of conversation in the bar was silenced as Dalgety strode over and ordered another beer. He drank it down in one go and stalked out for some air.

ONCE HE HAD CALMED down he realised that his temper had probably blown the mission. He was meant to befriend Heisenmatt, and instead he had shouted him down in the bar where he was having his lunch. Not good. He quickly decided that Vermont need never know about the episode.

Dalgety spent the afternoon putting off going to Heisenmatt's shop to collect the camera. He felt humiliated enough by his failure without having to endure another scene with the German, but without the camera he could hardly explain to his colleague that the whole idea had been absurd from the start.

At five-thirty he pushed the door open and the little bell tinkled. After a moment Heisenmatt appeared.

'Aha. It is you,' he said.

'Listen,' Dalgety began, vainly hoping to recover acres of lost ground. 'I really should apologise ...'

'My dear sir, it is I who should apologise to you. I have been so upset about the World Cup I have utterly forgotten my manners. Allow me to close up the shop and buy you a drink.'

Dalgety's mouth dropped open in astonishment. The little German busied himself rapidly turning out lights and locking cabinets and minutes later they were in the bar becoming firm friends.

'So you are a football fan?'

'Indeed yes,' Jim replied enthusiastically.

'Who is your team?'

'Heart of Midlothian.'

'Aha. Heart of Midlothian, from Edinburgh, I think?'

'That's it.'

'The Hearts. Their shirts are ... maroon, yes?' Dalgety nodded, and swigged his beer. 'And last year they miss the championship on goal average.'

'Aye!' Dalgety growled, remembering the taste of that day.

'To ... Kilmarnock. But the great rivals are Hibernian of Edinburgh. Hibernians versus Hearts. There is a game I would like to see.'

'Aye, well make sure you go to Tynecastle. Easter Road's a toilet.'

'Myself I follow Schalke 04, of Gelsenkirchen. That is where I was born. I like to make films of the games.' Heisenmatt mimed using a cine camera with his hands. 'Not good films, of course, but for fun.'

The two men grinned at each other, and drank beer in the international fellowship of football.

'Actually I use a Canon 200 like yours,' Heisenmatt went on. 'What do you think of it?'

'It's ... OK ...' Dalgety had only used the thing that morning. 'What about you?'

To Dalgety's relief Heisenmatt began a long discourse about the merits of various home movie cameras, and didn't ask him for another opinion until the conversation had worked round to football again.

The German held forth on the subject of the World Cup final the week before, and revealed that he had travelled to London for the match. Dalgety explained that Scotsmen would rather anyone won the Cup than England, and described the taunting and gloating that he had been subjected to in his office. Both men agreed, as the evening wore on, that it was the worst thing that had happened to them in years.

'I wouldn't mind so much,' said Dalgety, 'but that third goal was a travesty, a scandal. Never mind that the fourth goal should never have counted. There were people on the pitch, dancing around, putting the keeper off.

That third goal, though. Cah! It was never in. It should have been two–two, should have been a replay.'

The bar was empty now, except for the two men and a barman wiping down the tables. Heisenmatt was silent, looking at Dalgety with a thoughtful expression on his face.

'I suppose we'd better ...' Dalgety slurred, waving a hand to indicate that they should maybe leave.

'Come with me, Jim,' Heisenmatt said, 'back to the shop. I want to show you something.'

'OK, Wolf,' Dalgety agreed, suddenly sobered by the recollection that he was on a mission.

The two men walked, a little unsteadily, back to the camera shop. As Heisenmatt fumbled with his keys, Dalgety caught sight of a plain white car parked a few yards down the street on the opposite side. His practised eye spotted the two men sitting in the darkness, and he realised with a start that the shop was under surveillance. This meant it was reasonable to assume that somebody else was after whatever it was he and Vermont were after.

He followed the German through the shop and into the room at the back. It was a storeroom, with boxes of equipment and films stacked against the walls, that doubled as an office and a sort of living room when the shop wasn't busy. A door with a red light above it clearly led to a darkroom, and another to the staircase up to the first-floor flat where Heisenmatt lived.

'Sit, sit,' Heisenmatt said, ushering Dalgety towards a comfortable-looking frayed old armchair.

The German bustled around, first to a fridge to get a beer which he thrust into Dalgety's hand, then shifting some boxes away from the wall to leave a large whitewashed expanse. He uncovered a cine projector and aimed it at the wall. Then he removed a painting and leaned it against his desk. Dalgety's heart skipped a beat as he saw that Heisenmatt had revealed his safe, and he watched carefully to try to memorise the combination, which the German was making no effort to conceal.

'I think you will appreciate this, Jim.'

Heisenmatt took a film from the safe and loaded it on to the projector. Dalgety thought to himself that whatever he was after would most likely be in the safe, which Heisenmatt had left open, so he stood to stretch his legs, and managed to peer inside. To his astonishment there was nothing in there at all.

'Now, watch this!' Heisenmatt said, and started the film.

VERMONT WAS WAITING for him when Dalgety got back to the hotel just after one in the morning. 'Where the hell have you been?' he hissed, careful not to wake other guests despite his anger. 'You were supposed to report at 1800. You've been drinking, I can smell it. I told London you were working on the case and couldn't report in, but that's the last time I'm covering for you.'

'I was on the case,' Dalgety protested. 'I've been drinking with Heisenmatt. He's quite a good bloke, actually.'

'Oh, really?' The righteous rage Vermont had been building up for seven hours deflated. 'You might have let me know.'

'Yeah, sorry.'

'So have you gained his confidence, what do you think?'

'Yeah, I suppose so.'

'And do you think you can trust him?'

'I don't see why not.'

'Well, that being the case, London has authorised me to brief you on the item we are here to retrieve.' Vermont paused, savouring his little moment of importance.

'Yeah, about that. Whatever it is, it's not in his safe. And there are two goons watching his place. Are they ours?'

Vermont's blank look answered Dalgety's question.

'OK, what is it, the item? Perhaps we can work out who they are.'

'Oh, well, it's apparently a piece of cine film of the World Cup final.'

Dalgety gaped at Vermont in open astonishment.

'Heisenmatt was there, evidently, right on the goal line among the press photographers.'

'He told me. He got a pass from a friend on *Die Zeit*.'

'Right, there you are. He took this film, which he claims shows categorically that Hurst's second goal didn't cross the line. So what, right?'

Dalgety ground his teeth.

'Except that Heisenmatt went to see Werner Roth, the president of the German FA, last week, told him that the German nation had been cheated, and demanded that he ask for the match to be replayed. Roth agreed with him, and called the minister for sport, which is how we got to hear about it.'

'Huh?' said Dalgety.

'Bonn station routinely taps all members of the German government, obviously.'

'What, even the minister for sport? In case the Germans are planning a massive expansion of their playing fields programme into the Sudetenland, presumably?'

Vermont snorted. 'You may scoff, but discussions have been going on at the very highest level both here and back home.'

'I can't believe we've been sent here to hush this up,' Dalgety said. 'So they demand a replay, the English can just say no, can't they? The referee's decision is final, and all that?'

'The feeling is that, if placed on the spot, the British government would have to back a German call for a replay in the interests of détente. It's not a pleasant choice, though.

'Either way relations between Britain and Germany would become severely strained, not to mention relations between the government and the electorate. Far better not to have to make the choice at all.

'So we're here to get hold of the film, and any copies of it, and destroy them.'

'I see.' Dalgety frowned. He realised he was too drunk to think clearly. 'I'm for bed, I think.'

'OK, Jim,' said Vermont. 'Tomorrow, you go and see Heisenmatt again. Find out where he's got the film, and if there are copies, and take it from there.

Good night.'

THE FOLLOWING MORNING Jim Dalgety had his customary breakfast cigarette watching the Mosel and the Rhine joining and flowing away to the north. He could see the hotel on the far side of the Platz, and noticed Vermont, clad in gaudy plus-fours, climbing into a taxi, off to spend the day on the golf course.

Dalgety thought about what Vermont had told him the night before. The more he turned Heisenmatt's little scheme over in his head, the more merit it seemed to have.

A replay of the disastrous World Cup final, and the smile wiped off smug English faces. What could possibly be more desirable than that, in fact? The question was, how to bring it about without getting a black mark on his career file ...?

He decided against going to the shop straight away. The two heavies in the white car had already had a look at him, and there was no sense in making his interest in Heisenmatt any more obvious than it already was. It occurred to him that he might have acquired a tail of his own, so he spent the morning climbing the huge rocky hill on the other side of the Rhine and looking around the deserted fortress at the top which commanded such a marvellous view of the town and the surrounding countryside. If anyone followed him he didn't see them and at least they'd be knackered.

He knew where Heisenmatt would be at lunchtime, and strolled back into town to meet him, accidentally on purpose, in the bar.

'Ah, Mister Hearts!' Heisenmatt greeted him, 'Mister Jam Tarts!' He waved Dalgety over and called for a beer. 'How did you like my little film show last night? Interesting, eh?'

Dalgety nodded.

'I'm afraid your camera is kaput, my friend. I need a part, a little wheel, which cannot arrive before next Friday and surely nobody can holiday in Koblenz for that long! Tell you what, though. I have a second-hand camera which is similar. I'll swap it with yours and when yours is fixed I keep it. OK?'

'That's very kind, Wolf,' said Dalgety. 'Now listen. There's something I need to talk to you about ...'

The German's face darkened into a frown as Dalgety told him that he was an agent for the British Secret Service and that his mission was to dispose of the World Cup film. Heisenmatt was alarmed to hear that men were watching his every move, but Dalgety calmed him down. 'They're probably to protect you from me,' he said. 'They're nothing to do with us, anyway.'

'OK Jim, I will trust you,' Heisenmatt said. 'We are friends, because of football, yes?' Dalgety nodded. 'And I know we both want the same thing, the replay. What must I do?'

'I can buy you a bit of time. You must get the film to your contact at the German FA as quickly as possible. Arrange to hand it over in person. Is there only one copy?'

'At the moment, only one,' said Heisenmatt, thoughtfully.

'I understand. Don't tell me any more. Meet me tonight at eight in the square where the rivers meet and tell me what is happening. OK?'

'OK, my friend,' said the German and he slugged down the last of his beer and scurried out of the bar.

JIM DALGETY LEANED back in his chair and took a deep breath. It seemed to Neil Pettinger that the Scotsman had reached a part of his tale that he was going to find it hard to tell. He leaned over and took his visitor's mug and made him another cup of tea.

THIS TIME when Vermont returned from his golf Dalgety was waiting for him. 'Jim. How'd you get on with our krauty chum?' asked Vermont. 'Fine.'

'Did he mention the film at all?'

'Not yet. I need a couple more days to get him to relax and trust me. I'm sure he'll tell me all about it.'

'Good, good. I'll pass that on to London. Care to join me for dinner?'

'Er ... no. No thanks. There's something I need to do this evening.' As Dalgety left for his own room, he failed to see the faintly quizzical expression on Vermont's face.

LATER, IN A HOT BATH, Dalgety allowed himself the luxury of imagining Wembley packed to the roof once again for the replay of the World Cup final. Hurst's hat trick expunged from the record books, Bobby Charlton perhaps sidelined with a hamstring injury, Banks suffering from food poisoning, Moore – who knows? – implicated in some bizarre shoplifting scandal ... No, that was going too far. The match, second time round, a big disappointment. The English players fuelled by resentment, the Germans by righteous indignation. Alf Ramsey's team talk: 'You've won it twice, now go out there and win it a third time!'

After eighty-nine gruelling minutes, Beckenbauer pumps the ball into the area. Banks comes to meet it, Seeler goes up, Moore goes up and the ball glances off the England captain's head through the keeper's hands into the unguarded net. England players fall to their knees. Jack Charlton bursts into tears. Alan Ball grabs the ball from the back of the goal and runs to the centre circle to kick off. He taps it to Hunt and ...

'PEEEEP!' Dalgety blew the final whistle on his fantasy and threw his head back and laughed.

Heisenmatt was waiting for him in the square.

'It's all fixed. I spoke to Roth and told him what you said, that the British government would have to support a replay if the demand came from the highest level. He's very excited. I'm making the handover at noon tomorrow, right here in Koblenz, in the Platz.'

Dalgety smiled. He felt that a huge weight had been lifted from his shoulders. The two men shook hands and went their separate ways. As he walked into the hotel, the Scotsman didn't notice the rifle-microphone being withdrawn from the upstairs window-sill.

THE FOLLOWING MORNING Vermont found Dalgety reading a three-day-old copy of *The Times*. It was the first time since the final that the Scot had been able to bring himself to look at a sports page and he was just allowing himself a wry cackle at speculation that Alf Ramsey would get a knighthood in the next honours list. 'Aye! In your dreams, Alfie boy ...'

'Morning, Jim. I'm just off to have another crack at this course. You seeing our chum Heisenmatt today?'

'I expect I'll pop round there later on. I don't want to crowd him, you know.'

'No, quite. It is important, this film, you know, Jim. I hope you know what you're doing.' Vermont's eyes narrowed in the bright sunlight.

'Oh aye, son. Don't worry about me.'

Vermont nodded slowly, then shrugged and turned away. Dalgety watched him go and rehearsed his story in his mind as he did so. 'Sorry, Vermont. It seems Heisenmatt has already handed over the film to the German FA. We're too late. There's nothing we can do ...'

Just before noon Dalgety peered through a little hole he had torn in *The Times* – it amused him, when the heat was off, to play parody secret agent – and spotted his friend the little German camera-shop owner making his way along the far edge of the Platz towards the promontory at the point where the rivers met. He looked nervous but determined and his hands were thrust into his pockets as if, Dalgety thought, to make absolutely sure the precious film couldn't escape by itself.

Heisenmatt leaned against a railing, awkwardly feigning casualness and his eyes darted around the open square. It wasn't crowded. Local office workers with their sandwiches would start appearing in half an hour or so, but now there was just the odd knot of tourists watching the barges and a few retired folk out for a stroll in the sun.

Heisenmatt checked his watch and Dalgety found himself doing the same. The minute hand clicked round to twelve and Dalgety heard a church clock nearby begin to strike midday.

His gaze swept the square and he spotted two men in dark raincoats making their way purposefully towards Heisenmatt. 'Here we go,' Dalgety said to himself. 'Very punctual, your Germans ...'

One of the men was in his forties and stockily built. Dalgety decided that this must be Werner Roth, the administrator, as the other man was lithe, lean almost, and maybe twenty-five.

They reached Heisenmatt and Dalgety saw introductions being effected. While the stocky chap did the talking, the younger man stood behind the shopkeeper, hands in pockets, his gaze sweeping the square slowly from side to side. Dalgety found himself admiring the efficient way they were covering each other and then a nameless panic suddenly gripped his bowels.

He flung the newspaper aside and jumped to his feet. He walked forward slowly, disbelievingly, as he realised what was troubling him. This pattern that the two Germans in dark raincoats had adopted, this didn't look like two ordinary desk-job men, sports administrators, conducting a simple transaction; this was textbook security agent teamwork.

Heisenmatt took the spool of film from his coat pocket and handed it to the stocky man, tapping it to emphasise what he was saying.

'No!' Dalgety shouted, breaking into a run. 'No!'

The stocky man shook Heisenmatt's hand and turned away. Heisenmatt smiled and offered his hand to the other one. The second man took his hand from his pocket, crossed in front of Heisenmatt and seemed to punch him, fast and hard, in the stomach.

Dalgety pelted desperately across the Platz, reaching for the gun he always carried in a holster under his armpit, but he wasn't close enough yet to fire. As Heisenmatt doubled up in surprise and pain, Dalgety saw the sunlight on the long red knife in the younger man's hand.

'No!' he screamed again, cannoning in his haste against the corner of a bagel stall.

Stocky glanced quickly around the square and nodded to his colleague, who suddenly bent down, grabbed Heisenmatt by the ankles and pitched him over the railing into the river. The two men nodded at one another, drew their dark raincoats tight around their waists and strolled nonchalantly away.

Only Dalgety had seen what had happened. As he galloped towards the killers, gun first, they saw him coming and broke into a run. Dalgety got one wild shot off. People scattered, screaming. There was another shot, but Dalgety knew he hadn't fired it. He felt the bullet burning through his thigh and he sprawled on the flagstones, gasping for breath, weeping with impotent fury.

He lifted his head to see the two dark raincoats disappearing into a white car and driving off with a squeal of rubber. Ignoring the pain in his left leg, Dalgety dragged himself to the promontory and clung to the railing, scanning the vast rivers below.

A little way off he finally caught sight of a dark shape, bobbing rapidly along in the mighty current towards, he supposed, Rotterdam. As he watched, the shape drifted in front of one of the massive coal barges heading downstream, which bashed it firmly under the surface and Dalgety never saw it again. His head dropped and tears of grief and frustration pricked his eyes. Then he realised he was not alone. Vermont was standing next to him, dressed, rather comically, as a bagel stallholder, wearing a white apron and a little green cap bearing the legend 'Der Bagelman'.

'You fool!', Vermont muttered, 'You utter, bloody fool!'

NEIL PETTINGER looked at his kitchen clock and saw to his astonishment that it was past midnight. The white-haired Scot opposite hadn't spoken for five minutes now and was staring sorrowfully at the bottom of his mug. Neil wondered if the story was finished. He knew he had the makings of a book, if only he could tease the answers to one or two questions from his guest without getting shot. He hadn't forgotten the gun which Dalgety had pointed at him, oh, eight hours ago now, but was in no doubt how important the film was to Dalgety and reckoned that the Scot needed him.

'Listen,' he said, 'you can stay here tonight if you want. We can get the film from the shop in the morning.'

'Thanks lad, that's good of ye,' Dalgety said.

'One thing I wanted to know, though ...' Dalgety raised an eyebrow. 'Which one of them shot you? The stocky one or the young one?'

'Ach! Don't ye understand? It was Vermont. Vermont shot me, the bastard.'

DALGETY LAY ON HIS BACK and stared at the ceiling. He heard Vermont to his left but didn't look at him. 'You know you're finished, of course, don't you?' Dalgety said nothing. 'As soon as you're able to walk I'm to take you back to London. I'm not to let you out of my sight until we get to Strowger's office and then you'll be damn lucky if they don't chuck you in prison and throw away the key.'

'What the hell for?'

'Treason, I shouldn't wonder. We've straightened out the German police – eventually – but Strowger's another matter altogether.'

'Why did they have to kill him? Eh?'

'If you'd done your job properly Heisenmatt would still be alive.'

Dalgety had worked this out for himself, but it still hurt to hear it out loud. He turned to the Englishman sitting beside his hospital bed. 'Vermont, will you do me one favour?'

'I suppose I owe you one. For the leg,' Vermont shrugged.

'I'd like to go to the funeral.'

A couple of days later the two British agents stood at the graveside of the German camera-shop owner. Under some trees at the far side of the cemetery, Dalgety caught sight of two men in dark raincoats, watching.

The brief service finished and Dalgety hobbled with the aid of a walking stick over to the grieving widow.

'Frau Heisenmatt?' he ventured. 'I was a friend of your husband.' He thought to himself, 'Some friend. I never even knew he was married.'

Heisenmatt's wife smiled and took his arm.

'Thank you so much for coming,' she said. 'You must come with us to the shop. There is sherry and some food.'

Before Vermont could intervene, Dalgety clambered into a car with Frau Heisenmatt and was whisked away. He glanced over his shoulder and saw his colleague curse and sprint over to their hired car to follow.

'His body was found more than twenty miles away, you know.' Frau Heisenmatt said, matter-of-factly, as they drove along. 'That's practically halfway to Cologne.'

At the shop, Dalgety knew he only had a minute or two. 'Frau Heisenmatt?' he said. 'Wolf and I were both such great fans of football. I wonder ... could I perhaps take one of his films to remember him by?'

'Of course, of course. They are all in a box through there. Help yourself.' Frau Heisenmatt drifted away to start handing round sherry and small snacks.

Dalgety stumbled quickly round the counter and through to the back room. He was almost certain that Heisenmatt had understood the need to make a copy of the film – but where had the German hidden it? Thirty seconds' work opened the flimsy safe, which was empty, as he half-expected.

Dalgety turned his attention to the box of Heisenmatt's cine films. Where better to hide it than in here? He quickly checked the labels and all were 'Schalke 04 v Kaiserslautern', or 'Schalke 04 v Karlsruhe'. It could conceivably be any one of these ... He pulled one out of its case and held a strip of film up to the light. He could just make out tiny blue and white figures on a green background and slung it back in the box.

He checked nearly all the films before he saw Vermont through the doorway, nudging past the funeral guests towards him and defeat tasted bitter in his mouth.

'Come along, Jim. Time to go.'

IT WAS THE GERMANS, of course,' Dalgety explained, as he helped Neil Pettinger spread sheets and blankets on the spare bed. 'Vermont heard us arranging the handover and the Germans intercepted his report to London. Their government was afraid that a fuss like we were going to cause would ruin Anglo–German relations for years and their plan was to get Britain into the bloody Common Market, where they'd have us by the balls, as you know. Their Secret Service was ordered to hit Heisenmatt and Vermont was ordered to make sure I didn't cock it all up.'

'I see,' Neil murmured, handing Dalgety a pillow.

'Twenty-nine years it's been and not a day has passed in all that time without me thinking of him. My fault ... If I'd only ... Ach!' Dalgety sat on the edge of the bed. 'The quarter final in 1970. Wolf would have loved that. And they won the thing in '74, of course.'

'And 1990,' Neil said.

'And do you know, from that day to this, Hearts haven't won a single trophy?' Neil did know, naturally. 'A judgement, that's what it is. A judgement against me.' The Scot fell silent again. After a while Neil asked, 'What happened when you got back?'

'They slung me in a safe house for a year. Not prison exactly, but as good as. When they let me out I went to Koblenz, of course, but Frau Heisenmatt had sold up and gone who knows where. I knew no one had found a copy of the film, though.'

'How?'

'A friend in the Service looked at the reports for me. And the more I thought about it the more I thought I knew what he'd done.' Dalgety held the old envelope up in front of Neil's face. 'He posted it to himself, didn't he? Didn't arrive till after the funeral. Canny little bugger, Heisenmatt was.'

THE FOLLOWING MORNING Neil woke early. He made himself a coffee and began scribbling down in a notebook as much of Dalgety's story as he could remember. He'd almost finished when he heard the Scot coughing his way through the first cigarette of the day. A moment later the man himself appeared in the kitchen doorway. 'Come on, son. I'll buy us breakfast in the café over the way.'

'One thing still puzzles me,' Neil said, as they made their way down the communal staircase to the street. 'When you've got the film, after all these years, what are you going to do?'

Dalgety told him. Neil stopped in his tracks and a low whistle escaped from his lips.

In the café Neil munched a bacon sandwich and watched Dalgety tucking into fried eggs, mushrooms, sausages and fried bread. He felt the dénouement of his book slipping away from him.

'Are you absolutely sure kidnapping Graham Kelly is the best plan?' he asked.

'Hmmm? Don't you think I can do it?' retorted Dalgety.

'Oh no, I'm sure you can kidnap him all right. I'm just not that sure they'll be bothered enough about getting him back to do what you want.'

'You got a better idea, son?'

'As a matter of fact,' said Neil, leaning over the table and lowering his voice, 'I have ...'

That evening QPR were due to play Nottingham Forest in the third round of the Cup. Two hours before the kick-off Neil presented himself at the main entrance at Loftus Road. A uniformed commissionaire held the smoked-glass door open a fraction and peered at him.

'Hi,' Neil said. 'My name's Neil Pettinger and this is Jim Dalgetybridge. We're the statisticians from Sky TV.' He'd said the magic words and the commissionaire let them both in. They made their way up to the mini-studio with windows looking out over the pitch.

A youth with headphones and a clipboard hushed them as they came up the steps and they heard Richard Keys, the Sky anchorman, recording a trail for that evening's live broadcast.

'Tonight, live and exclusive on Sky Sports,' Keys was saying, 'action from the third round of the Littlewoods-sponsored FA Cup. Two of the First Division's big guns, Queens Park Rangers and Nottingham Forest, begin their quest for this, the most famous trophy in world football.'

The presenter turned and patted the F.A. Cup, which was on the table beside him. 'Join us for all the action, tonight at seven!'

'OK, Richard, that was fine. Break, everyone!' said a voice and the studio emptied. Neil peeked around the door and then said to his companion: 'OK, Jim. I'm going with them for my alibi. There's just the one Group 4 man in there with the Cup.'

Dalgety grinned. Neil trotted down the stairs to make sure plenty of people saw him having his polystyrene cup of lukewarm tea.

He was on tenterhooks for half an hour or so, but he needn't have worried. The rudimentary security of a top football club was no match for the fieldcraft of a Secret Service agent, even if it had been thirty years since Dalgety had used the neck pinch or smuggled anything over a high wall. Finally Neil – and everybody else – heard the producer shout: 'What do you mean it was the real one?! What happened to the fucking replica one?'

'Stolen last time, I'm afraid,' said a voice.

GRAHAM KELLY, the chief executive of the FA, took the phone call later that evening. He listened to the Scots-accented voice on the other end of the line, then asked: 'How do I know you've really got the Cup?' A pause, then he heard the clanking of the lid being placed on the famous old trophy. He ground his teeth.

'All right. What is it you want?'

He listened to the instructions, his eyes widening with astonishment. 'Oh, this is madness!' he exclaimed. Then, as more metallic clangs came down the phone,

'All right, all right, you swine. I'll do what you want. Just don't hurt it!'

TEN DAYS LATER a cold wind swirled around the twin towers of Wembley Stadium; an occasional flurry of snow was carried along horizontally, never really threatening to settle. A middle-aged man and his ten-year-old son stood outside the entrance; a young woman barred their way.

'What do you mean there's no tour today? We've come

down from Sheffield for this, you know?' the man said.

'I'm sorry, sir. Why don't you try the London Dungeon?'

'I wanted him to see where we won the World Cup. I was here, you know, that day ...'

'Yes,' thought the woman as she closed the door on them. 'You and four million of your mates.'

Out on the famous pitch a couple of dozen middle-aged men stood in groups of three and four, stamping their feet to keep warm. Neil Pettinger moved among them with a camcorder, recording some seriously grim expressions.

Sir Alf Ramsey was there, his mouth a hard line, his eyes cold. Geoff Hurst, Martin Peters, Gordon Banks, Alan Ball and the Charlton brothers stood together.

'Bloody get on with it,' Jack Charlton muttered as Neil walked past.

Jim Dalgety wandered along the goal line at one end, until he found the spot from which Heisenmatt had filmed his telling home movie.

The ten English players and the nine Germans that the FA had succeeded in reuniting had watched in silence as Dalgety ran the film in one of the executive boxes.

As Hurst's shot cannoned down off the crossbar they could all see that the ball did not cross the line and a collective gasp shivered around the room.

Only Beckenbauer had spoken.

'I knew it!' he'd cried, leaping to his feet and pointing. 'I knew it!'

Dalgety hugged the memory, then looked at the sky.

'You thought that was good, Wolf? Now watch this!'

He walked briskly over towards the Royal Box and waved a signal. A burly security man disappeared down one of the passages behind the box and returned accompanied by a slight elderly lady. The Queen.

Flanked by Graham Kelly and Charles Vermont, now deputy chief of the Secret Service, Her Majesty made her way to the centre of the front row and picked up the small gold Jules Rimet trophy, which had been flown in from Brazil the night before.

The England players climbed the steps slowly and filed past the trophy barely looking at it.

'At least Mooro isn't here to see this,' one of them muttered, as he collected from Graham Kelly his specially struck medal with the single word 'Loser' on it.

Then Beckenbauer, nominated captain for the day by the German party, led his former team-mates up to the Royal Box.

'Many congratulations,' the Queen said, not really understanding what she was doing there.

Beckenbauer took the trophy, kissed it and held it high over his head while his team-mates grinned and applauded.

Dalgety raised his fists above his head and laughed.

If...

Maradona had been sent off for deliberate handball

THE 1986 WORLD CUP was the apotheosis of Diego Maradona. His prodigious skills dominated the tournament from beginning to end and his brilliant goals against Belgium, England and Italy are seared into the memory.

The single most memorable moment of the tournament and sadly for him of his fantastic career, however, was the one in which he rose to meet a miskicked clearance by Steve Hodge in the England penalty area and, realising that he could not beat Peter Shilton with his head, used his fist to put the ball into the net.

Despite the fact that his second goal, four minutes later, was one of the greatest seen on the world stage, it is the first that will be remembered most vividly and which devalues his claim to be the greatest player of all time.

Maradona had had to deal with fame and adulation from an early age. As a seven-year-old he had appeared on Argentinian TV juggling oranges with his feet – and oranges weren't the only fruit – he also used to do various other ball-juggling tricks as half-time entertainment at League matches.

It is difficult to say whether there is a British equivalent of Maradona's achievement in moving from half-time entertainer to international star without knowing whether David Beckham was ever one of the Sky TV sumo wrestlers, but I suspect there isn't.

Maradona played his first full season at the age of sixteen for Argentinos Juniors, helping them to promotion, and was first picked for the national side as a seventeen-year-old. He narrowly missed out on selection for the 1978 World Cup squad, but Argentina didn't drop him again until forced to by FIFA's routine dope testers in 1994.

He won a championship with Boca Juniors

That famous picture of the punching scandal. Shilton aims for Maradona's head ... and misses.

To entertain the crowd at half-time, Maradona takes on – and beats – Dougie Squires and the Younger Generation.

Maradona had it all, from immaculate diving to sublime skill.

before arriving in Spain for the 1982 World Cup as Barcelona's latest signing. There he was brutally treated by Italy's Claudio Gentile, who whacked him in the face, and by most of the Brazilians, who kicked and chopped and niggled away at him until he studded one of them in the chest and was sent off.

For a time it seemed that Maradona would not be allowed to realise his full potential. The Spanish League proved a harsh arena and one tackle by Andoni Goicoechea, who gloried in the nickname 'The Butcher of Bilbao', ruptured his ankle ligaments and left him with three steel pins in his leg. The Butcher keeps the boot he made the tackle with in a glass case in his living room. Alongside a bumper from his car that he once killed a dog with. Lovely bloke.

Terry Venables, Maradona's new manager, decided that Barcelona wasn't big enough for both of them and unloaded Maradona to Napoli, replacing the world's greatest player with Steve Archibald. Astonishingly, Venables was Barcelona manager for a further two years.

In Naples Maradona was lionised. Sixty thousand fans turned up to watch his first training session – an informal one which consisted of half a lap of the pitch and a couple of lines of coke – and he lifted the ordinary southern team onto another level. He did the same for his national side. The 1986 Argentinians were an unexceptional bunch, but with Maradona urging, creating and scoring for them they were contenders for the Cup.

Argentina topped their opening group, beating Bulgaria and South Korea and drawing with Italy. They then dispatched Uruguay in the second round to line up their quarter final with England.

England's progress to that meeting started smoothly enough. They were the only European team to qualify unbeaten and had big wins over Finland and Turkey. Northern Ireland qualified second in England's group at Romania's expense after picking up their last vital point in a 0–0 draw at Wembley. Kerry Dixon missed two sitters, which had the Romanians muttering about a fix, but they clearly hadn't ever seen him play before.

Robson's injury inadvertently turned his namesake into a good manager.

England should have been confident, on the crest of a wave of good form, but morale was dented by the release of their weediest ever World Cup single. 'We've got the Whole World at Our Feet' was neither as toe-tappingly catchy as 1982's 'We're on Our Way', nor as hip as the England/New Order anthem would be four years later. It wasn't even as funny as a Kevin Keegan single. It was just piss poor. Really, really piss poor.

Once England began their Group F campaign in Monterrey the wheels came off. Bobby Robson's 4–3–3 formation relied too heavily on the ball-winning skills of his captain and namesake Bryan, who was far from fully fit but whose name the manager was confident of spelling properly on the team sheet.

At twenty-nine, Bryan Robson should have been at his peak. He had long seemed irreplaceable in the national side, with his abilities as a tackler, motivator and finisher making him England's one world-class player. Unfortunately he had missed half of the season for Manchester United through knocks, firstly a bad hamstring injury and then a dislocated shoulder.

Ron Atkinson, the Manchester United manager, postponed the operation that would have put the shoulder right in time for the World Cup so that Robson would be available for his club right to the end of a season in which they finished fourth, a long way off the title pace.

In a warm-up game in Los Angeles against Mexico, Robson fell awkwardly and his weak shoulder popped out again. This meant that playing him in the World Cup at all was a calculated risk, but without his captain Bobby Robson's tactical plan would have to be completely altered, so a special harness for the weak shoulder was constructed.

For the opening match against Portugal, Robson and his harness played in a three-man midfield with Ray Wilkins and Glenn Hoddle. Chris Waddle, Gary Lineker and Mark Hateley were the strikers, as Bobby Robson stuck to his plan to use a winger and a big target man. The defence in front of Peter Shilton consisted of Terry Fenwick, Butcher of Ipswich, Kenny Sansom and Everton's Gary Stevens. For seventy-five minutes England were in control, but then Portugal scored with their first attack and England finished the match in panic and disarray.

When England played Morocco things got even worse. Robson's enormous bandage bra proved worthless as his shoulder dislocated itself again and he left the field in the thirty-eighth minute. Moments later Wilkins followed after a disagreement with the referee over the difference between throwing the ball to and throwing the ball at.

England held on for a 0–0 draw and Bobby Robson, deprived of two key midfielders for the last match through injury and suspension, was forced to tinker with his system. In came Steve Hodge, Peter Reid and Trevor Steven alongside Glenn Hoddle in a revamped 4–4–2 formation, with Lineker partnered up front by Peter Beardsley.

Against Poland England were revitalised and ran out easy 3–0 winners, with Lineker scoring the hat trick that he says represented the real start of his international career. Bobby Robson had stumbled on a team that worked almost at the last possible moment. Reid and Beardsley were international new-comers, but both managed to reproduce their club form when it mattered. The same team, with Alvin Martin in for the suspended Fenwick, hustled past Paraguay 3–0 in the next, knockout round and prepared to meet Argentina in the quarter final.

England v Poland, Monterrey. A Lineker hat trick from a combined total of seven yards.

**World Cup quarter final, 22. 2. 86
Azteca Stadium, Mexico City**

Even the players
had to queue
for tickets.

THE TEAMS

ENGLAND
Shilton, M.G.Stevens, Butcher, Fenwick, Sansom; Hoddle, Reid (Waddle), Hodge, Steven (Barnes); Beardsley, Lineker.

ARGENTINA
Pumpido, Cuciuffo, Brown, Ruggeri, Olarticoechea, Batista, Giusti, Burruchaga (Tapia), Enrique, Valdano, Maradona.

HALF-TIME ARRIVED in the '86 quarter final without any serious goalmouth incident, as the English midfield tried to stifle Maradona and the Argentinians strove to cut off the supply to Lineker and Beardsley.

Five minutes into the second half the deadlock was broken by 'that goal'. Maradona ran at the English defence, strung out along the eighteen-yard line. His attempted lay-off should have been hoofed into touch, but Hodge lobbed it back over his own head towards Shilton. Maradona followed through to challenge the keeper, but it seemed Shilton must just punch the ball clear. Suddenly, in the blink of an eye, it was bobbling into the net and Maradona was wheeling away to celebrate. On the replays it was

obvious what he had done and you could catch his guilty glance at the ref to see if he had been spotted. The ref, however, had been deceived by the speed of the action, as had the linesman. It seems incredible, given the number of snappers who managed to capture that exact milli-second, but there you go.

As though inspired by the goal to prove that he could score a proper one, Maradona shimmied past Beardsley, Reid, Fenwick and Butcher to score a great second and the game was more or less up for England.

'You have to say that's magnificent!' cried Barry Davies, neglecting to mention that you had to say it through gritted teeth.

Bobby Robson sent on Barnes and Waddle, reverting in a last desperate throw to his beloved wingers and they almost pulled it

The Hand of God (unseen) opens the scoring.

off. Barnes tricked his way past the tiring full-back with ten minutes left and whipped over a perfect cross which Lineker nodded in.

Minutes later Barnes provided a carbon copy of the cross, which Lineker, straining, just couldn't reach. Perhaps if he had stuck out a hand he could have nudged the ball in and how different things would have been if he had.

You can imagine how animatedly Maradona would have pursued the ref to get the 'goal' disallowed and if Gary had claimed it, as Maradona so shamelessly had his, then it would have blown Lineker's Mr Clean image for ever.

Who knows, maybe, seduced by the dark side of the Force, Lineker's career would then have been littered with bookings and sendings off and rather than becoming the 'Queen Mother of Football' he would have turned into Ian Wright. Or Roy Keane. He would no longer have been the housewives' favourite and he could have kissed bye bye to his media career. (Oh *why* didn't he do it...?). He would probably now be a hairdresser in Leicester. Or a chiropodist.

After the match Maradona declared that the controversial goal had been scored by 'The Hand of God', thereby allowing the English press to get worked up about blasphemy for the first time since 1690.

England and Bobby Robson went home with more dignity and credit than had seemed possible a few short days earlier and Gary Lineker was acknowledged as one of the top strikers in the world, winning the prestigious Golden Boot and three tins of special golden dubbin.

Maradona meanwhile single-handedly – although actually on this occasion he did use only his feet – won the semi-final against Belgium with two brilliant goals and Argentina met West Germany in the final.

The Germans used their best player, Lothar Matthaus, to shackle Maradona, but although their star was quiet, Argentina went two up through Brown and Valdano. Rummenigge and Voller levelled the score, before Maradona, twisting in the centre circle, sent Burruchaga clear for the winner.

Bobby Robson said, 'Arsenal could have won the World Cup with Maradona', like his successor gravely over-rating the talents of Martin Keown.

Diego Maradona was at the pinnacle of his career. The fact that his triumph and Argentina's was tarnished by his cheating didn't seem to bother him unduly and he swaggered through the following season with Napoli, taking them to the double.

The blind adulation of the Neapolitan people – some white, some pink, some brown – meant that Maradona was given leeway to conduct himself pretty much as he pleased. He would miss the start of the Italian season to go fishing and he threw himself into Naples' seedy nightlife with enthusiasm.

He started to find getting up in the morning to train didn't suit him – he was always a big fan of *Richard and Judy* – so Napoli switched training to the afternoons and although he and the club had a disappointing 1988 they were riding high in 1989 when Maradona's form suddenly tailed off.

The strong local feeling was that the Argentinian's acquaintances in the Neapolitan underworld had supposedly bet against Napoli for the title and this suspicion was not allayed by the consolation prize of the UEFA Cup.

Napoli took the title again in 1990, but Maradona came to the World Cup in Italy overweight and carrying a number of injury problems. He had a large blood clot on his foot and needed an operation to have cortisone deposits from previous pain-killing injections scraped from his ankle. He was only able to show flashes of his best form.

Argentina tottered unconvincingly to the final, where they lost a terrible game to West Germany. Before they beat the hosts Italy on penalties in the semi at Naples,

One-man team.
Maradona competed for
the Serie A title under
the name Napoli.

Maradona tried to persuade the locals to support Argentina, saying, 'Napoli no es Italia'. That was the end of their love affair with him and the following season he was voted 'Most Hated Man in Italy' in a news-paper poll, finishing ahead of Saddam Hussein.

He left Italy in 1991 after a series of fines, disappearances, retirements, a court case during which his involvement with drugs and prostitution became known, a paternity suit and finally a fifteen month ban for failing a dope test. Brief comebacks at Seville and in Argentina followed, before a popular clamour restored him to the national side in time for USA 94.

There a further routine dope test failure ended his career in ignominy and disgrace.

But what if... Diego Maradona hadn't got away with the handball in '86?

THE WORLD CUP *quarter final. England v Argentina. Half-time arrives with neither goalkeeper seriously tested. The English midfield are concentrating on stifling Maradona, while the Argentinians block the supply to Lineker.*

Five minutes into the second half Maradona surges at the England defence. His pass to the right goes astray and Hodge hooks the ball high into the England penalty area. Shilton comes out to punch it clear, but before he can make contact Maradona flicks it into the net with his fist. The little Argentinian wheels away to claim the goal, while the English players vehemently protest that it is handball. The Tunisian referee is not quite sure what he has seen and goes to consult his linesman.

Meanwhile Maradona is leading his teammates in a jubilant celebration nearby. When he sees the referee point to award a free-kick in the England area he holds his head and falls to his knees in theatrical disbelief. The referee then strides over to him and shows him the yellow card for ungentlemanly conduct.

There is uproar. Every single Argentinian surrounds the referee and they jostle him threateningly and expertly, making sure the official can't tell which of them is man-handling him at any one time.

Then Maradona, tears of frustration streaming down his face, thrusts himself to the front of the throng and as he pleads his case for the goal he shoves Ali ben-Naceur in the chest. The Tunisian stumbles and falls to the ground.

There is no mistaking the guilty party and Maradona is sent from the pitch. Chaos follows for several minutes. First Maradona refuses to leave, claiming that the ref has been felled by 'The Hand of God', then the entire Argentine team seems about to leave with him, unwilling to allow Diego alone in the changing room with their valuables. Carlos Bilardo, the Argentine manager, gallops on to the pitch and is restrained by FIFA officials.

Eventually calm is restored and the match resumes without Diego Maradona. The news cameras of the world follow him as he

Could these
have been
English hands in
1986?

is ushered, tearful and disbelieving, down the tunnel.

Without their star playmaker, Argentina go to pieces and Olarticoechea, the Butcher of Buenos Aires – a man who led listeners in Britain to believe that Barry Davies was saying, 'Oooh! I'll take a chair!' – is required to do just that, sent off for a hacking challenge on Beardsley.

Bobby Robson sends on an extra attacker, John Barnes, to take advantage of their disarray and he lays on the only goal of the game for Gary Lineker ten minutes from time.

ARGENTINA	0
ENGLAND	1
Lineker 80	

SO BOBBY ROBSON'S *England*, vilified at home only a few days earlier, found themselves in the semi-finals of the World Cup. Better still, most of the classy-looking opposition had got itself knocked out. The dangerous Danes had come unstuck in the second phase against Spain, who themselves had gone out on penalties to Belgium. The Belgians, England's semi-final opponents, had also taken care of the Soviet Union in a 4–3 thriller, while France had disposed of Italy and Brazil.

The fluent attacking play, centring around Beardsley and Hoddle, which had destroyed Poland and Paraguay, was seen again to great effect in the Belgium game. England won 3–1 with goals from Lineker, Beardsley and sub Chris Waddle. Alf Ramsey had suggested in the press that Waddle's true worth to the squad lay in the fact that they could take sausage meat with them which Waddle could make up into sausages in Mexico as required.

The Germans, who had looked uncon-vincing in the tournament so far and who had had by far the easiest run to the semis, having beaten Morocco, Mexico and Scot-land, beat France 2–0 to set up a re-run of the 1966 final. Franz Beckenbauer, the West German manager, insisted throughout that his team were not good enough to win the trophy and who are we to argue with a man of his standing?

World Cup final, 29. 6. 86
Azteca Stadium, Mexico City

ENGLAND WON *the toss to decide which team would wear their favoured white shirts in the '86 final, so, unlike in 1966, the Germans lined up in green.*

Scotland manager Alex Ferguson warned that the Germans would be difficult to see in green. Robson retorted that the one team he knew he wouldn't be seeing in the final was Scotland.

In the days leading up to the final Bobby Robson was rumoured to be considering a recall for Bryan Robson, who had been experimenting with other harnesses for his shoulder, including one that encased his whole torso in plastic which was later to form the basis of the costume design for Robocop. Robson tried to convince FIFA to permit this by saying that it was a bullet-proof vest and that the captain had received death threats – but they recognised Don Howe's handwriting.

After a cagey first half, England surged into a two-goal lead early in the second half. Gary Lineker finished a flowing move involving Steven, Hodge and Beardsley with a tap-in from about two feet out and a Glenn Hoddle free-kick from the edge of the area curved into the top corner leaving Schumacher flailing helplessly.

Although the Germans pulled one back through Karl-Heinz Rummenigge, England held on, bolstered by the appearance of their skipper with fifteen minutes to go. Bryan Robson lifted the side's morale at a crucial time and the four-minute hold up as he was carried off on a stretcher destroyed the Germans' concentration at a vital time.

When the final whistle went, Robson was determined to lift the World Cup and he did, momentarily, before the weight of the little gold statuette popped his shoulder out again.

These, then, are the names that children chanted in playgrounds up and down the country.

THE TEAMS

ENGLAND
Shilton, M. G. Stevens, Butcher, Fenwick, Sansom, Reid, Hoddle, Steven, Hodge, Beardsley, Lineker (Robson 76, G. A. Stevens 82).

WEST GERMANY
Schumacher, Berthold, Briegel, Jakobs, Forster, Eder, Brehme, Matthaeus, Allofs, Magath, Rummenigge.

ENGLAND 2
Lineker 49, Hoddle 56
WEST GERMANY 1
Rummenigge 70

● A record television audience of 29 million watch the final. The streets are empty and in years to come everyone can remember where they were, what they were drinking and who they were drinking it with. Except for Jonathan Aitken, who thinks he might have been in Paris with his daughter, or in Switzerland with his wife, or somewhere else.

● Scottish psychiatrists report a huge upturn in business, with cases of depression at an all-time high.

● Football, so down in the dumps in the previous year after the Bradford disaster, the Heysel tragedy and the mental behaviour of Millwall supporters at Luton, gets an enormous lift. Attendance figures for the following season are hugely up and people who had never previously given football a thought begin to discover the game, rapidly becoming diehard fans.

● The sport becomes trendy overnight and all the papers carry articles by literary figures about how they were converted to football by this World Cup. A number of books are published on the theme of 'How I've always been a big football fan only I kept really quiet about it.' One of these, *Hot Stuff* by Twyford-born Chris Turnbull, becomes a bestseller, telling an autobiographical tale of a nerdy lad in his thirties and his lifelong love for Tottenham Hotspur – apart from when he was at university and supported Oxford United.

The trappings of success. Diego in his luxury bedsit.

● Meanwhile, Reading-born Nick Hornby pens a tome about his love for Arsenal culminating in their League Cup final defeat by Luton. Most critics agree that this isn't much of a climax.

● England's eight-goal hero, Gary Lineker, transfers to Barcelona for £2.75 million. He makes a fortune endorsing the humorously named 'Sal y Lineker Patatas Fritas'.

● Diego Maradona is utterly chastened by his experiences in Mexico. He is despondent at having let his country and his people down and feels the shame keenly. He realises that he has missed the chance to stamp his name for ever on football history and determines to win the World Cup in 1990.

● He dedicates himself totally to football, leading a monastic lifestyle, eschewing the temptations offered by the Neapolitan nightlife. He becomes a fervent anti-drugs campaigner. He leads Napoli to four Scudettos and his team-mates gratefully guzzle the lovely chocolate-covered nutty ice cream. Then, having got their attention, he leads them to four championships and to two European Cup wins, arriving at Italia 90 with the calm certainty of a man preparing to meet his destiny. Argentina, fired by Maradona's motivational skills and his prodigious talent, sweep all before them and take the World Cup. Maradona is man of the tournament.

● He returns to Argentina to open a coaching academy, where he trains boys from all backgrounds, selflessly spending hours on end showing them how to juggle various types of fruit with their feet. He dedicates himself to ensuring that the boys will all have a successful career once they leave his academy and sure enough Maradona's All-Boy Fruit Juggling Troupe become a much sought-after half-time entertainment the world over.

● In 1987 the first 'Boys of '86' documentary hits British TV screens, charting the ups and downs of the World Cup winners since their triumph in Mexico.

Maradona
agreed to a live
televised debate
with Shilton.

As they are all still playing professional football this is not particularly revealing.

● Bobby Robson is fêted as England's greatest – and luckiest – manager, the first European to win a World Cup outside Europe. He receives a knighthood in the New Year's Honours List and a two-year respite from back-page headlines calling for his head. England qualify comfortably for Euro 88 in Germany, but there they crash to ignominious defeats against Eire, Holland and Russia and the sniping begins. At least they don't have to qualify for Italia 90.

● England, as holders, kick off the 1990 World Cup against little-known Cameroon. They crash to a shock 1–0 defeat, even though the Africans are reduced to nine men, after two are sent off for crude hacking tackles on Lineker and Gascoigne. Bryan Robson is ruled out of the rest of the tournament after dislocating his head. The Lions of Cameroon are fêted throughout the world for their exciting attacking play and become the darlings of the tournament

everywhere except England, where they are decidedly the villains of the piece and are dubbed the 'Camer-loons' by the *Sun*. In the second phase Cameroon's tiny support is swelled by thousands of Scots, who attach themselves to the African side after their own has gone home early. Again.

● England lose in the second round to the brilliant Brazilians, who eventually finish runners-up to Argentina in a memorable, Maradona-dominated, final. Robson pays the price for being too loyal to his 1986 team, as two own goals by Terry Fenwick see England knocked out.

● Sir Bobby Robson gives way to Graham Taylor and it is the end of the road for some of the heroes of '86.

● Robson, knighted in 1987, is relieved of his knighthood under the Conservative government's new 'Knighthoods are for winners' scheme. In his place a knighthood goes to Phil James, the 1990 *Stars in Their Eyes* champion of champions. He goes to the ceremony as Fish out of Marillion.

If... ID cards had become compulsory for football fans

IN 1985 **MARGARET THATCHER** was looking for a scrap. She'd led a firm to take the Argies in the Falkland Islands and defended her manor against the mighty coal miners, destroying the troublesome coal industry to boot. Now, like any barking mad pub brawler, she was just waiting for someone else to look at her pint.

Football and in particular, football hooliganism, chose this unfortunate moment to become the hot news item on all the front and back pages and, like Nero confronted by the Christians (the early religious cult not the pop band) she thought to herself, 'I can have these!'

Although hooliganism had been a continuous problem in the English game for many years, in the early eighties the incidents seemed to be increasing in frequency and ferocity. In the previous season there had been disturbances at matches between Middlesbrough and Leeds and Chelsea and Brighton, in which fans and police had been injured. Spurs were fined eight grand by UEFA after their fans ran amok in Rotterdam

and riots marred England's international visit to Luxembourg. The fans there eschewed the offered excursions to the financial district in favour of the more traditionally English pursuit of putting the windows through in the local bars.

Heindrich Schwarz even threatened to ban British clubs from Europe unless the government acted to prevent hooligans travelling abroad. This didn't concern the football authorities too much, as Herr Schwarz was a farrier from outside Munich. However, they had to take notice when UEFA general secretary Hans Bangerter threatened to ban British clubs from Europe unless the government acted to prevent hooligans travelling abroad.

Then on 13 March 1985 Luton played Mill-wall in a televised FA Cup quarter final. Suddenly the hooligan problem that had remained at anecdote's length for most football supporters was there on the box for everyone to see .

Hundreds of Millwall fans tore up plastic seating and hurled it on to the pitch. They

The truly unacceptable face of
hooliganism: hooligans who can't
fight properly.

The woman who
loved football.

charged down after it and used it as weapons and shields in a running battle with 200 policemen.

The referee took the players to the dressing rooms for twenty-five minutes while the police cleared the pitch, but the rioting continued after the match in Luton itself, with thousands of pounds of damage being done in a rampage that gave the town centre a much-needed facelift.

Thatcher ordered football's top brass to Downing Street to explain themselves. Ted Croker, secretary and chief buck-passer of the FA, called out, 'Number 37 ... Swansea City!' from force of habit and then tactfully added, 'These people are society's problem. We don't want your hooligans at our sport.'

The government's response was to pass a bill banning the sale of alcohol at football grounds – not that anybody seriously believed there was any alcohol in the piss-water football clubs passed off as beer – and to begin plans for a national identity card scheme. The idea being that it would be impossible to gain admittance to a football match without an ID card, which could then be withdrawn from troublemakers, who would be dumbfounded by this move, too stupid to fake a new one or steal one from somebody else.

These rudderless ships would then drift into some other activity like painting or carpentry and a new England would emerge, optimistic, self-sufficient. Summers would be longer and those who insisted on watching football would be sent to live in Wales.

Although the ID card scheme was widely perceived to be unworkable, the Heysel disaster in June gave the move added momentum and Thatcher was persuaded that it was the way ahead. This in turn convinced two of her toadying supporters to begin plans for their own schemes in advance of the national

Innovative, football-loving visionary, or self-seeking, reactionary half-wit? Only time has told.

plan, like a pair of pain-in-the-arse kids handing their homework in early.

Ken Bates announced that Chelsea would be starting an ID scheme, erecting an electric fence to keep fans off the pitch and banning the press from Stamford Bridge in the mistaken belief that it was journalists who were kicking it all off. All these initiatives proved to be too bonkers to work, but gave us all an insight into Mr Bates' attitude to his 'customers'.

Meanwhile the chairman of Luton Town, David Evans, a man as popular as he was attractive, instigated a ban on away fans at Kenilworth Road which was to be enforced using a very expensive computerised ID scheme for home fans.

The first home match under the new system was against Southampton. To the great amusement of the world at large the computerised turnstiles proved slow and unreliable and hundreds of fans missed Luton's fourth-minute opening goal.

A group of West Ham fans trample a BBC documentary crew underfoot.

The rows rumbled on throughout the 1986–7 season. Luton chose to withdraw from the League Cup rather than relax their ban, which contravened the rules of the competition and at the end of the season the scheme was quietly dropped.

Thatcher, however, doggedly clung to her insistence that a national ID scheme should one day be introduced.

Gradually, she came to realise that it was not just football supporters who were complaining about it, but sensible well-educated civil rights campaigners as well.

After the Hillsborough tragedy in 1989 the emphasis switched to safety and Thatcher was able to continue to insist that football get its house in order by upgrading its facilities and so on, although the ID card plan was eventually scrapped.

In any case hooliganism was a diminishing phenomenon and all-seater stadia reduced the ease with which fans could congregate en masse and make a nuisance of themselves.

The trendy gentrification of the game in the nineties transformed the media's perception of the typical football fan and Thatcher's successor was keen to be seen to be a Chelsea supporter at every available photo-opportunity – stopping short, however, of butting Helmut Kohl in the face and saying, 'That's for the blitz, Fritz.'

In the end the problem, like its extravagant solution, simply went away.

But what if...
a compulsory national ID scheme for football fans had been introduced?

● Ignoring howls of protest from the press and civil liberty campaigners, Thatcher introduces a compulsory ID card scheme for football supporters. It will be in place for the start of the 1987–8 season.

● It will be impossible to gain entry to any match in the Football League, the FA Cup or the Football League Cup without a card, which will carry a passport-style photograph and other information on a magnetic strip. Unless you bung the bloke on the turnstile twenty quid.

● There is a minor political storm at the outset of the scheme when it is discovered that Mark Thatcher has bought a large stake in 'Photo-Me booths UK Ltd.'

● Supporters have to apply for their cards from their home clubs and many find that the cards take at least four weeks to arrive. Thatcher cannot see that this is a problem, saying, 'We have to buy tickets for the opera six months in advance.'

● Manchester United's first home game of the season, against Arsenal, attracts a crowd

of under 12,000, but thousands more demonstrate outside the club's offices to complain that their applications have not been processed yet.

● This pattern is repeated all over the country and attendances for the first month of the season are down to a third of the equivalent for the previous season. Thatcher declares that these are teething problems and that once the system has settled down everything will be fine.

A bloke without an ID card is forced to hang around in a public bog to see the game.

In a desperate attempt to lure fans back to football, clubs would run competitions in their pro-grammes like this one: 'Can You Spot Anthony Booth out of *Till Death Us Do Part?*'

● By Christmas, however, things are even worse. It seems that every week brings news of a fresh ID card riot at a football fixture, caused often by fans with legitimate cards being denied entry to a match because of some computer error. Football violence reaches an all-time high.

● UEFA threatens to bar England from the 1988 European Championships, for which they have just qualified with a thrilling 4–1 win in Yugoslavia. Thatcher declares she might withdraw the national side anyway.

● Casual football supporters complain that they can no longer go to a match with a friend who supports another team. They find they are separated, herded off with away supporters or, more frequently, denied entrance altogether. Their bleating was largely ignored on the grounds that they were a bunch of part-timers and deserved it.

● Into the New Year and the winter postponements, together with severely reduced gates brought about by the ID card scheme, cause severe cash-flow problems for a number of clubs. Newport County announce that they will be unable to fulfil their fixtures and a dozen other clubs are only weeks from taking similar drastic measures. Thatcher says this trend proves the scheme is working, since if the number of professional clubs is reduced, then the size of the problem is reduced, naturally. 'It's just like the mines,' she says, cheerfully.

● In one mid-February week thirteen clubs go to the wall. Doncaster Rovers, Hereford, Halifax Town, Aldershot, Hartlepool, Scarborough, Mansfield Town, Chester City, York City, Port Vale, Torquay United, Reading and First Division high-flyers Millwall all admit that they can no longer carry on. Violent demonstrations take place at all of them, except Port Vale where fans are sidetracked by the bargains on offer at Vale Market.

● In the aftermath of these riots and with more clubs in danger of going bust at any time, the police say they can no longer cope. Thatcher declares a State of Emergency and creates a combined police/army task force, to be known only as 'The Task Force', which will be given special powers to deal with the problem.

● Away fans are summarily banned, and all males are prevented from going further than thirty miles from their homes on Saturdays. Manchester United go bust.

● UEFA kick England out of the European Championships. With English football in disarray, many top players announce that they are no longer prepared to play in their own country and take lucrative contracts to play in Scotland where the game is thriving. Top English clubs are under so much pressure financially that they are forced to allow their stars to leave at bargain basement prices.

All sports seemed to lose their sense of fun. Here, the horses line up for the 1987 Grand National.

Hibs' poor form really aged the devastated Proclaimers.

● Football fans who were unwise enough to acquire ID cards to watch their teams now find that businesses have access to a database with all the information they have supplied on it. Fans discover to their horror that they can no longer get credit, mortgages, or insurance of any kind as a result of having declared an interest in football. They also have to report to a police station every forty-five minutes, making games virtually impossible to attend.

● Forty-eight consecutive editions of *The Time, The Place ...* are devoted to the ID cards issue. A peaceful march is organised by the Football Supporters' Association to bring their grievances to the attention of the government.

● Two hundred thousand people join the march, filling Whitehall and Trafalgar Square. The Task Force charge them, attempting to disperse the crowds using tear gas, horses and hitting with big sticks. There are many casualties.

● Thatcher goes on television to denounce the Football Supporters' Association as a subversive political organisation. It is declared illegal and hundreds of ringleaders are arrested in dawn raids by The Task Force. Many vociferous protesters appear on the television to express their outrage at this

move, including the leaders of the opposition parties and Amnesty International. They are arrested in dawn raids as well.

● In a shock broadcast, the Home Secretary declares that ownership of a football supporter's ID card is now an illegal act, and since everyone who owns one supplied their name and address in order to get it in the first place, thousands more arrests follow.

● Unemployment figures show a massive improvement, since the incarcerated don't count as unemployed.

● Wembley Stadium can no longer be used for the Cup final or internationals because it has become a makeshift prison

compound, where hundreds of thousands of football supporters are held against their will by armed guards and forced to pay through the nose for nasty beef-burgers and soggy chips. Wembley Stadium officials are criticised for trying to sell prisoners glossy souvenir programmes of their incarceration at £10 a time.

● The imprisoned supporters seem remarkably well-behaved, sporadic outbreaks of the chant 'Let us out, let us out, let us out ...!' being suppressed by baton charges.

● Thatcher appears in public at the head of a column of tanks. She is riding a horse and seems to be wearing a suit of black armour.

She organises a rally in Trafalgar Square, which is attended by many thousands of her followers, delighted by the downfall of football. They rejoice that they will now no longer have to waste so much time tutting and writing letters to the council trying to have planning permission blocked for new football grounds.

● With her strident voice echoing off the walls of the National Gallery, Thatcher proclaims that she has won a great victory over football. The League season has ended in disarray, more than half the clubs in the country have gone bust and next season has been declared illegal. She further announces the cancellation of the next General Election.

● In a rerun of the infamous 'night of the long knives', Thatcher expels from the Conservative Party anyone with any form of connection to football. Kenneth Clarke, a Nottingham Forest fan, is thrown in jail, while John Major and David Mellor both strenuously deny any affiliation with Chelsea FC.

● 'I've never been to Chelsea,' Major said, while pop star Elvis Costello reiterated that he didn't want to go to Chelsea either. Nobody seriously believed that David Mellor was a football supporter in any case, so he was safe.

If...Waddle had scored against Germany then ... Gazza might have led a normal life

AH, ITALIA 90. The summer dominated by the haunting strains of 'Nessun Dorma', Puccini's enchanting aria recounting a family holiday in Scotland in a Volkswagen camper.

The penalty shoot-out that decided the England–West Germany semi-final in that World Cup is seared on to the memory of all who saw it and there was a record televison audience watching. Only the last episode of *The Thorn Birds* comes close, apparently and that was because the *Sun* misprinted it as *The Porn Birds*.

Which of us, plunged into depression by that most heartbreaking of defeats, has not since imagined what it would have been like if only the Germans had missed a couple of their penalties, instead of Pearce and Waddle missing ours? There'd have been a deeply unsuccessful allegedly humorous Pizza Hut advert on last year, for one thing, featuring Gareth Southgate, Andreas Brehme and Karl-Heinz Riedle.

More satisfying, though, to think of Waddle clinching a genuine winner in extra time with his raking shot from the edge of the area, which in real life cannoned out off the post to safety and crying, 'The sausages are on me!'

Argentina were ripe for the picking in the final, having sneaked past shattered Italy in a penalty shoot-out – which curiously had an identical sequence of events to our one – the night before.

With Caniggia, their most dangerous forward, suspended and Maradona unfit and showing only glimpses of what he was capable of, England would never have a better chance to pick up a second World Cup to go with Geoff Hurst and Kenneth Wolstenholme's one from twenty-four years before.

England's finals campaign had, like the one in 1986, got off to a stuttering start. The 1–1 draw against Eire, though a disappointing result to a terrible match, wasn't a mortal blow. The format of the tournament meant that the group stages only eliminated eight teams and it was possible to go through finishing third in Group F.

Matthaus makes
Waddle feel
even worse by
patronising him.

Gazza in full flight was one of the World Cup's enduring memories.

(Below) Bobby Robson waits for a bus to take him back to the team's Sardinian hotel.

For the second game against Holland, Bobby Robson apparently succumbed to pressure from the players to use a sweeper system and it worked well.

Mark Wright was the third centre-back behind Terry Butcher and Des Walker and England had the better of the 0–0 draw, with Gascoigne showing precocious skills, including one turn past two Dutch defenders that Johan Cruyff would have been proud of. As in 1986, however, Bryan Robson picked up a serious injury, this time to his ankle.

A Mark Wright header clinched a 1–0 win over Egypt which saw England through to the second round, where Belgium were to be the opposition. This match was illuminated by one inspirational moment, which represented the real start of David Platt's career as an international.

In the last minute of extra time, with the score 0–0 and the match heading for penalties, Gascoigne was brought down by Gerets forty yards out. Gazza appeared to be contemplating a shot at first, but then chipped into the area where Platt watched the ball drop over his shoulder, then swivelled and smashed an unstoppable volley past Preud'homme for the winner.

Never had ex-Stoke boss Mick Mills' refusal to sign David Platt seemed to sum up his 'loser' image so well.

In the quarter final against Cameroon, England were seven minutes from a 2–1 defeat when a Gary Lineker penalty rescued them and a repeat in extra time sent them through to their date with the Germans.

For the semi-final, the biggest game of his managerial career, Robson sent out the team most England supporters wanted to see.

Indeed he'd picked a squad few would quibble with except those in charge of the Esso World Cup coin collection. Butcher would be the free man at the back this time and Waddle joined Gascoigne and Platt in an attack-minded midfield.

FOR HALF AN HOUR on 4 July in Turin England ripped into the Germans. Gazza brought a good save from Illgner at the foot of a post, but although territorially dominant, England created few good chances. By half-time Germany had come back into things and the game was in the balance.

THE TEAMS

ENGLAND
Shilton, Parker, Butcher (Steven), Wright, Walker, Pearce, Platt, Gascoigne, Waddle, Lineker, Beardsley.

WEST GERMANY
Illgner, Brehme, Kohler, Augenthaler, Buchwald, Berthold, Matthaus, Hassler (Reuter), Thon, Voller (Riedle), Klinsmann.

David Platt ensures his England place for another five years.

Just before the hour the Germans took the lead. Pearce fouled Hassler on the edge of the box. Thon rolled the free kick to Brehme and Paul Parker charged from the wall to close down the shot. The ball looped up off Parker's leg and Shilton, inexplicably advancing – perhaps he'd caught sight of a bookies', I don't know – was caught out.

He stumbled as he tried to get back, fell on his arse and watched helpless as the ball spun over him into the net.

England equalised ten minutes from time. Parker's cross bobbled between Kohler and Augenthaler and Lineker suddenly found himself with a chance, which he raked past Illgner into the bottom corner.

Early in extra time, Chris Waddle smacked a low shot from the edge of the area. As it passed the keeper it looked a goal, but the ball bent away and rapped the post.

Gascoigne then, who had been singled out for special attention and was fouled more times than a London footpath, lost control of the ball and as he reached for it he brought down Thomas Berthold.

It was barely worthy of a free kick, but as Berthold rolled in 'agony' and the German bench screamed and pointed their protests, the referee reached for the yellow card. This meant that, should England reach the final, they would be deprived of their new star through suspension and the tears that would make Gazza a household word flowed.

To his credit he pulled himself together and produced some driving attacking play which threatened to create a goal, but it was Buchwald who came closest to resolving the issue with a shot that thumped Shilton's left-hand post.

Lineker, Beardsley and Platt scored their penalties for England in the shoot-out and Brehme, Riedle and Matthaus replied. Then Stuart Pearce hit Illgner's legs, Olaf Thon scored and Chris Waddle skyed England's last hope way into the night.

The Germans won the World Cup, of course, but in a disreputable final from which Argentina's Monzon and Dezotti were sent off, and which was decided by a decidedly dodgy Brehme penalty.

England returned home to a heroes' welcome and Gazza found that his tears had elevated him overnight to cult icon status.

Lineker cracks home an eight-yard thunderbolt to level the scores in the semi-final.

The trendification of football had begun and a West End hit play – *An Evening With Gary Lineker* – sprang from the bitter disappointment of that semi-final night.

It dealt with a fantasy reality in which England won the penalty shoot-out, Stoke City won promotion and various other crazy things happened.

But what if... Waddle's shot had hit the post... and gone in?

THE ENGLAND PLAYERS pile on top of Chris Waddle in celebration, as Germans stand around, dejected, stunned, efficient and well-disciplined. As Waddle jogs back to his own half for the kick off, Gascoigne attempts to ruffle his new lucky short spiky haircut and cuts his hand.

Bobby Robson is on the touchline, urging his men to concentrate, to hold on to the lead. 'Do I like that,' he cries. West Germany drive forward. Klinsmann beats Shilton with a header, but it comes back off the bar. Gascoigne clatters Berthold right in front of the German bench, but despite their protests the referee only awards a free kick. Gazza grins.

For the second half of extra time Robson brings on defender Gary Stevens for Lineker. He goes to right-back and Parker moves into the middle in a new defensive formation.

The seconds tick away and, just as it seems the referee is about to blow, Guido Buchwald unleashes a last-ditch effort from thirty yards that rattles the post and spins away for a goal kick.

Shilton ambles slowly after the ball, but the final whistle goes before he can retrieve it.

The final in Rome, four days later, is thus between England and Argentina. The press make light of the history of enmity between the nations when it comes to the Falkland Islands, but no one has forgotten or forgiven the Hand of God, or the dumpy little bloke it was attached to.

Sublime skills from Waddle
helped blot out memories of
his 1986 haircut.

The cast of the conspicuously unremarkable *An Evening With Chris Waddle*, which flops on the Edinburgh Fringe.

Bobby Robson sends out the same starting line-up that he used in the semi-final and the match itself is a scrappy, violent affair. The Argentinians seem intent on spoiling and launch some savage attacks on Gascoigne in particular. One of these results in a red card for Pedro Monzon.

The single goal that wins the Cup, however, is very special. Waddle, the hero of the semi-final, picks up a loose ball near the centre circle and, spotting Goycochea off his line, lashes the ball from forty yards in off the underside of the bar. It is a goal destined for the title sequence of Grandstand *forever.*

● The England team return to a huge welcome at Luton airport. Gascoigne, voted one of the outstanding players of the tournament, is greeted raucously, especially as he appears to be wearing plastic false breasts, but the loudest cheers of all are reserved for Chris Waddle. The shy incomprehensible Geordie takes the adulation in his stride. Gascoigne's breasts turn out to be real and caused by 'refuelling problems'.

- Bobby Robson thinks about his future. In the build-up to Italia 90, tabloid sniping and the FA's unwillingness to commit to a new contract led him to accept a job as manager of PSV Eindhoven. Graham Taylor was appointed in his place. Now Bert Millichip comes under pressure from the tabloids to keep Bobby on and the FA is obliged to make him a vastly improved offer.

- Eventually Robson accepts and will lead England to Euro 92 in Sweden.

- Graham Taylor becomes manager of PSV Eindhoven. He finds it difficult to communicate with the Dutch players, as they all speak better English than he does. 'He says, "Do I not like that?" ' explains one exasperated player, 'but what does that mean? Does he mean he likes it, or that he doesn't like it? It is just nonsense.'

- Keith Curle, Carlton Palmer, Geoff Thomas and Andy Sinton never play for England.

- *An Evening With Chris Waddle* appears, almost unnoticed, on the Edinburgh Fringe. *The Scotsman* says, 'How did these mutts ever think a play about England winning the World Cup would be a hit in Scotland, for any's sake? A play about England *losing*, then you'd be talking …'

- Paul Gascoigne is an England regular after Italia 90, as England qualify for Euro 92 with ease. Gazza himself is calm and serene. He says, 'Winning the World Cup has just settled me right down. I used to be daft as a brush, me, but now I feel focused and fulfilled.'

- Gascoigne finds that he is under intense media scrutiny for a while, but once the press find that there is never any story to be had they leave him alone.

- Gazza coolly orchestrates Spurs' FA Cup win of 1991, before completing a straightforward move to Lazio, where he passes the medical with flying colours. He has given up drinking and so has his pal, Jimmy 'Three Bellies' Gardner.

- After three seasons as the darling of the Roman fans, Paul Gascoigne moves back to Newcastle United amid fears that he plans to start up the wild antics of his youth once again, but he says, 'I'm serious about this no drinking and so's Jimmy "Two Bellies".'

- At Euro 92 England reach the semi-finals where they meet Germany. After a 2–2 draw the Germans go through on penalties. Waddle is the unlucky English penalty taker, but afterwards he and Robson are philosophical. 'Some you win, some you lose,' they shrug.

- Robson decides to retire as England's most successful manager and Terry Venables takes over.

- As holders, England have already qualified for USA 94, so Venables has two years of friendlies ahead and then two more years leading up to Euro 96. Venables unveils his so-called Christmas tree formation, but says, 'There's plenty of time to experiment – next game I might try a monkey puzzle tree.'

- PSV Eindhoven are relegated from the Dutch First Division. A Dutch paper prints a picture of Graham Taylor's face super-imposed on a potato. The headline is an obscure Dutch pun about chips which doesn't translate into English very well at all. But essentially it's something like, 'If Taylor was a chip, you'd need sauce and even then he might not be very warm. Is this what we want?'

If... **Arsenal had failed to buy promotion after the First World War** *then...* **Barnsley would win the title in yellow boots**

ARSENAL IS NOWADAYS such a byword for probity and honesty, its players such models of sobriety and upright behaviour – not at all the sort of lads who would walk off with your luggage at the airport or steer their sports cars through your garden wall – that it may come as something of a surprise to learn that the legendary marble halls are founded on a piece of chicanery.

Long before Rune Hauge was so much as a twinkle in George Graham's wallet, the directors of Arsenal FC were at it. The North London giants proudly boast the longest consecutive spell in the English top division, going back all the way to 1919, but they should never have got there in the first place.

When football resumed properly after the First World War, the Football League decided to expand the First Division from twenty to twenty-two teams. They relegated the club that finished bottom in 1914–15, and then promoted three from Division Two. Not the top three, though. Oh no ...

The last Division Two table before the war looked very different to how we'd expect it to.

Arsenal skipper Mr Shaw slips Mr
McCracken, his Newcastle counterpart,
ten bob at the start of the 1919-20 season.

The great Herbert Chapman
conducts a piece of transfer
business with a Norwegian agent.

Division Two 1914-15

1. Derby County	53 pts
2. Preston North End	50
3. Barnsley	47
4. Wolves	45
5. Arsenal	43

Derby and Preston were promoted all right, but not poor old Barnsley. No, Arsenal were 'elected' to take their place among the élite, the coveted niche which by rights belonged to the South Yorkshiremen. And if you think those lads were bitter about it, spare a thought for Tottenham, the relegated bottom club passing Arsenal heading in the other direction.

What shenanigans went on there we may never know, but I have a strong suspicion that brown envelopes were involved in a transaction which probably took place in whatever passed for a Little Chef on the A1 in those days – possibly, knowing the pedigree of Arsenal men, the Back-stabbers Room at the Garrick Club.

Arsenal went on to great things in the years that followed – cheats, as we know, always prospering. They recruited Herbert Chapman as their manager, attracted by a CV that included three consecutive championships for Huddersfield Town, and, more pertinently, a ban for his involvement in making illegal payments to players while at now-defunct Leeds City.

Chapman, the Alex Ferguson of his day, was an inveterate tinkerer, especially when it came to Arsenal's kit. He it was who introduced the distinctive white sleeves on to the previously plain red shirts, and had his players play in blue-and-white-hooped socks 'to make them easier to see'.

As a player himself, Chapman had an even more extravagant solution to that particular problem, choosing to play his matches in lemon yellow boots.

Like Ferguson, too, Chapman presided over the most resented and unpopular team of his day. He was the first to instil a 'professional' attitude in his players, and his tactical masterstroke was to create teams that absorbed pressure for the vast majority of the match before winning with a single breakaway goal. This philosophy is somehow ingrained in the Highbury marble, subliminally adopted by succeeding generations of Gunners.

The plaintive cry of 'Lucky Arsenal' dates back to Chapman's tenure in the 1930s, and further resentment was caused by the club's conspicuous wealth. It was a time when the North – places like Barnsley, actually – was hit hard by the Depression, and Arsenal came to represent the affluent South and the all-round unfair state of things in the country.

Then there were championships and cups in each succeeding decade – except the sixties when they were mugged at Wembley by Leeds and Swindon – and European trophies too in 1970 and 1994.

Barnsley in the meantime have been forced to wait until 1997 – seventy-eight years late – to claim the place in the Premiership which should have been theirs by right, and the sixties and seventies were spent in Divisions Three and Four. If there's one consolation for Barnsley fans, it is that they didn't have to watch Willie Young.

Arsenal were 'elected' to take their place among the elite

But what if ...
Arsenal had been out-bunged in 1919?

Barnsley's David Seaman.

AT A PRESS CONFERENCE *to announce the recommencement of the Football League in the autumn of 1919, a* spokesman reveals, '*The First Division will be extended from twenty to twenty-two teams. Tottenham Hotspur will be relegated to Division Two, and promoted in their place will be Derby County, Preston North End and ... oh, excuse me, gentlemen ...*'

*A gentleman with a South Yorkshire accent asks if he can have a quick word, and a brief conference follows. Then the Football League spokesman continues his statement, '*Ahem ... and Barnsley. Thank you, gentlemen. Drinks and little sandwiches through the door behind you on the left.*'

The Arsenal representative, who looks not dissimilar to Dick Dastardly from Wacky Races, *slams a gloved fist into his gloved palm, mutters '*Curses!*' and storms off, slamming the door behind him, almost trapping the tail of his strange sniggering dog.*

Barnsley thrive in the top flight, and the club becomes famous around the world. The thrifty Yorkshire board balk at a proposal to construct an imposing entrance hall out of marble, using instead Blue John stone from nearby Derbyshire.

*This entrance hall leads to a passage with many confusingly unmarked doors off it, which a local '*confirmed bachelor*' describes as '*The corridor of uncertainty*'.*

Herbert Chapman is poached from neigh-

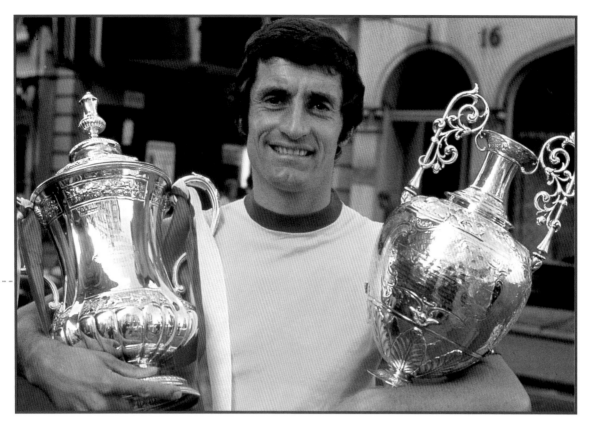

bours Huddersfield Town, attracted by being about twenty miles nearer to his home village of Kiveton Park in South Yorkshire. He leads Barnsley to three consecutive titles in the thirties.

Barnsley are widely resented for their success, especially in the South, where they are scornfully referred to as 'Lucky Barnsley'. Chapman changes their kit, adding distinctive white sleeves to their red shirts, but supporters – mostly from tough mining stock – demonstrate unsuccessfully to prevent the introduction of lemon yellow boots, preferring instead to suggest the use of pit helmets with lamps for night games.

Further successes follow as Barnsley record the longest unbroken spell in the First Division/Premiership. Highlights include the Fairs Cup win of 1970, and of course the double of 1971 which marked the high point of their bitter rivalry with Leeds in the sixties and early seventies.

Barnsley regain the title in 1989 and 1991, and local lad David Seaman is the hero as they take both Cups in 1993 and the Cup Winners' Cup in 1994. They are the first to experiment with a foreign coach – a Mercedes which they use to get to away games – and currently can field an entire first eleven of overseas players.

Arsenal, on the other hand, were confident that the promotion they were denied would come along. It was not to be, however, and they languished in the Second Division for a record forty-one years.

Relegation to the Third, and then the Fourth, Division was their fate in the sixties, when the one consolation was the occasional derby matches with fierce local rivals Orient. Better times have come in recent years, and finally Arsenal stand on the threshold of the top flight for the first time since 1913. The harsh realities of modern football, however, mean that a little club like Arsenal cannot realistically expect to compete with the giants of the game, like Newcastle, Liverpool and Barnsley, and they are the bookies' favourites for a swift return to their rightful lower rung on football's ladder.

Barnsley captain Frank McLintock shows off the 1971 League and FA Cup trophies.

If... Eric Cantona had signed for Sheffield Wednesday then... Trevor Francis would be a carrot

IT WAS A GOOD YEAR for football, 1991: Eric Cantona retired for the first time. His eight-year career in French football had seemingly ended in ridicule and opprobrium at a disciplinary hearing of the French Football Association.

A month earlier, while playing for his fifth club, Nîmes Olympique, against St Etienne he had taken exception to a refereeing decision, and had philosophically thrown the ball at the referee.

Cantona hadn't waited for the inevitable red card, but had strutted from the pitch to ear-splitting jeers from the crowd.

The disciplinary commission suspended the striker for four matches, informing him that they had taken into account his previous charmless volatile behaviour. This included punching an Auxerre team-mate in the face, calling Henri Michel, the French team manager, a 'shitbag', throwing his shirt at another ref while playing for Marseilles, and hitting a Montpellier team-mate in the face with his boots.

As he prepares to make his Sheffield Wednesday début against Baltimore Blast, Eric has a quick look round for Matthew Simmonds.

Cantona was not impressed by his punishment and in an ironic postmodern way, rather than in a spoilt little child way, went up to each member of the panel in turn to hiss 'Idiot!' in his ear. His ban was increased to two months on the spot, and Cantona retired from football immediately.

Not too many tears were shed in France, apparently; for Cantona, while a sublimely talented footballer, was also something of a figure of fun. His arty penchant for self-regarding pseudo-intellectual philosophising subsequently seemed glamorous and interesting to an adoring English audience, but to the French ear Cantona's thick Marseilles accent made him sound merely comical.

Imagine that thing about the seagulls following the trawler because they think that sardines will be thrown into the sea being said by Ian Rush, for example. Or the business in Cantona's Eurostar advert, 'Does the bird in a cage sing as sweetly as a bird who is free?' Suppose they'd got Mick Channon to do that one.

Is there no end to this man's talents? (Right) Putting on a tie. (Far right) Wearing a hat.

Think how you'd feel if you heard that the French thought Chris Eubank was really cool.

So. Eric Cantona in early 1992 was a washed-up joke figure in French football. None the less it did cause quite a stir when the then manager of Sheffield Wednesday, Trevor Francis, invited the Frenchman to make a comeback in English football and offered him a one-week trial at Hillsborough.

There were a few foreign players playing in the English first division at the time – Nayim, Kanchelskis, Hysen, Orlygsson and Limpar for example – and, in fact, for the first time the number of foreign imports exceeded the number of domestic players with drink-driving convictions.

Wednesday fans watched the sports pages with bated breath as the exotic and volatile star considered a new start in Sheffield, hoping against hope that their manager would take the risk.

Unfortunately the week of Cantona's trial fell in the middle of a typically grim English winter. Francis played Cantona in an indoor six-a-side game against American tourists Baltimore Blast, alongside Graham Hyde, Nigel Worthington, Chris Bart-Williams and Gordon Watson, but outdoor training proved impossible.

When the week was up Tricky Trev declined to offer Cantona a contract, instead suggesting a further week's trial, which the Frenchman refused from the vantage point of his remarkably high horse. Francis was not prepared to hire a player he had yet to see play on grass, for fear that he wouldn't be able to.

Thus the managerial opportunity of the decade was neatly sidestepped. Howard Wilkinson of Leeds United stepped in, gambling that Cantona would pep up his stumbling league leaders for the run in to the 1991-2 league title, and so it proved. Leeds finished four points ahead of runners-up Manchester United, and seven ahead of third-placed Wednesday. Then Wilkinson, inexplicably, off-loaded his new star to his greatest rivals, and the rest is Old Trafford history.

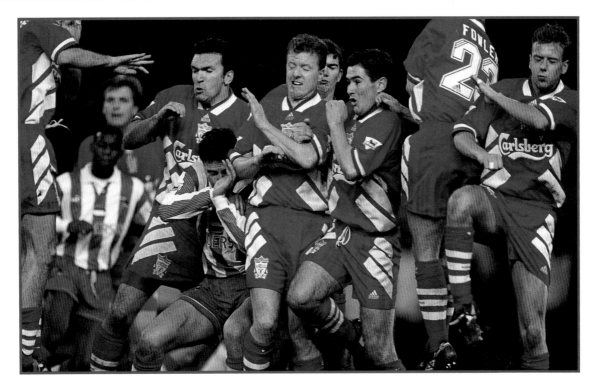

But what if...

Cantona had signed for Sheffield Wednesday in January 1992?

Liverpool went to extravagant lengths to mark Cantona out of the game.

● Suppose we say that Cantona's arrival gave Leeds a four points boost, and that little extra had instead gone to Wednesday. The top of the table would have looked like this:

1. **Sheffield Wednesday**   **79 pts**
2. **Leeds Utd**   **78**
3. **Manchester Utd**   **78**

The following season, Wednesday's championship side of Chris Woods, Roland Nilsson, Phil King, Nigel Pearson, Paul Warhurst, Carlton Palmer, John Sheridan, Danny Wilson, David Hirst, Eric Cantona and Nigel Worthington is strengthened by the arrival of Cantona's former Marseilles team-mate Chris Waddle.

● Wednesday go from strength to strength. Cantona is frustratingly ineffective in their European Cup defeat by Stuttgart, but is extremely influential at home. Wednesday

From the musical *Annie*: 'Steve Morrow, Steve Morrow, I've dropped you, Steve Morrow ...'

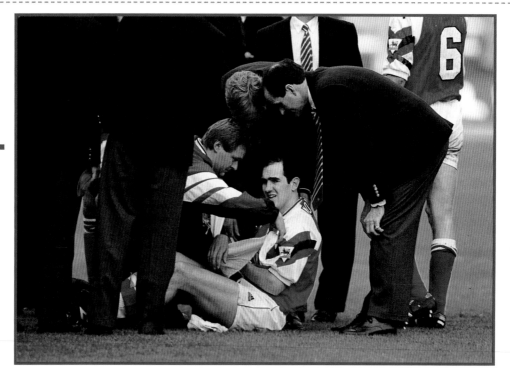

reach both Cup finals, coincidentally beating Arsenal in each, with Cantona scoring the winner both times from the penalty spot.

● Arsenal skipper Tony Adams is so annoyed by team-mate Steve Morrow's performance in the League Cup final that he picks him up and body-slams him on to the Wembley turf, fracturing the Irishman's collarbone.

● Wednesday also walk away with the League, leaving Aston Villa, Norwich City, Blackburn Rovers and a disappointing Manchester United trailing in their wake. Alex Ferguson complains that Wednesday have an unfair advantage, as blue and white shirts are easier to wash than red ones. Wednesday become the first team to win the Treble. Trevor Francis is Manager of the Year, Cantona is PFA Player of the Year and Waddle wins the Football Writers' Award.

● Cantona declares himself enchanted by the Sheffield arts scene. He is a regular at what he describes as 'the most exciting Dadaist festival in the world, where men dressed as waiters push perfect ivory globes around with long pointy sticks. The green tables are the fields of life,' he declares, 'and the erratic progress of the coloured spheres represents man's struggle against his very destiny. It's a bit like football, really.' The festival runs annually at the Crucible Theatre for a fortnight in April.

● His mentor is the local songwriter John Shuttleworth, whom he likens to Jacques Brel and in whom he discerns a hitherto unsuspected profundity, particularly in the songs 'Up and Down Like a Bride's Nightie', and 'My Austin Ambassador Y Reg'. Despite pronouncing himself flattered by Cantona's enthusiasm, Shuttleworth

John Shuttleworth and Alex Ferguson – two peas in a pod.

declines an offer to make a single with him, and Cantona instead taps the musical expertise and chart experience of team-mate Chris Waddle. Their duet 'Seagulls and Sardines' reaches number nine in what the youngsters refer to as the hit parade.

● Cantona's love affair with Sheffield is confirmed by his declaration of devotion for Sheffield crooners the Human League, although his Phil Oakey haircut is deemed to have cost him any number of goals from back-post headers.

● Fans of other clubs are irritated by his deep-thinking self-image, claiming anyone would think they were deep if they hung out with Carlton Palmer and David Hirst.

● Summer 1993. Manchester United, frustrated by their continued failure to capture the League title, dispense with the services of Alex Ferguson. He becomes manager of Galatasaray. His successor is Bryan Robson, who becomes player-manager.

● November 1993. England crash out of the World Cup despite beating San Marino 7–1 in their last qualifying game. Graham Taylor – dubbed 'Turnip' by the tabloid press – resigns, and the FA set about appointing his successor as England manager. Jimmy Armfield is commissioned to sound out opinion in the game at large, and a huge groundswell of popular support emerges for Terry Venables to take over.

The FA are, however, so enchanted to have an English manager who isn't Brian Clough in charge of the League Champions for once, that they unanimously hand the job to Trevor Francis.

One of the advantages of management is that you get a free programme.

Francis is in the difficult position of having only friendlies to play in the lead-up to Euro 96, and so defeats at Wembley by Greece, Nigeria, France, and Croatia are not seen as overly significant. There is widespread unease, however, at Francis' habit of bringing himself on as substitute to 'show them how it's done'.

Once Francis announces that he is going to try to emulate Jack Charlton's success at international level, and is discovered to have sounded out a number of Shelbourne and Distillery players to see if they have English grandparents, the honeymoon period is more or less over.

The tabloid press campaigns for his removal and, wanting to stick with the vegetable theme that proved so popular in its anti-Taylor campaign, while also remarking on Francis' resemblance to a well-known Birmingham comedian, decides that he is a carrot.

This is kinder than the verdict of the Wembley crowds at Euro 96, who take great delight in bastardising the Lightning Seeds and Baddiel and Skinner hit, bellowing 'He is a ****, he is a ****, he is a... Francis is a ****' throughout defeats by Switzerland, Scotland and Holland.

Is it Trev, or
is it ...?
You decide.

● December 1993. Sheffield Wednesday re-appoint Howard Wilkinson as manager. He decides that Wednesday's football is 'a bit fancy' and, in a shock move, suddenly sells Eric Cantona to Newcastle United for £175,000, saying that this is quite a good deal for a twenty-seven-year-old.

● 1994. Bryan Robson has a January sale at Old Trafford. Out go Schmeichel, Irwin, Bruce, Hughes, McClair, Ince, Sharpe, Kanchelskis and Giggs, although Clayton Blackmore is retained on a fifteen-year contract. They are replaced by four Brazilians, two Croatians, a Dane, a Latvian and an Albanian, for a combined outlay of £42 million. Two of them go missing within six weeks, complaining about the Manchester weather and saying that umbrellas should come with little instruction booklets. United are relegated.

● After two mediocre seasons in the second flight, the average crowd at Old Trafford falls below 20,000. The club shop calls in the receiver. Terry Venables buys the club for £1.

● Meanwhile, in Turkey, Alex Ferguson complains that Fenerbahce's kit is much nicer than Galatasaray's, which is the only reason for the fact that they look like taking the Turkish title.

● Cantona becomes a folk hero on Tyneside. Hundreds of fans copy his distinctive 'collar-up' style, previously only considered cool by the members of Buck's Flzz.

Terry Venables buys Manchester United for £1

● On the field he forms a lethal partnership with Andy Cole. Cantona scores lots of goals Andy Cole doesn't, but they share the driving to training. Newcastle win the League in 1994, 1996 and 1997.

● Blackburn take the title in 1995 as Cantona is forced to sit out six months of the season after jumping into the crowd at Selhurst Park to attack a fan. Giving evidence in his assault case, Cantona claims he had heard the man describe his acting début in an episode of *Spender* as, 'rather unconvincing and he was meant to be playing himself, wasn't he?'.

● He later makes his film début in *Le Bonheur est dans le Pré*. His performance is faintly praised by director Etienne Chatiliz, who says, 'His strong build gives power and credibility to the farmyard scenes.' Ahem.

● Although he professes himself drawn to the arts, he shows no sign of retiring again just yet and his merchandising operation is in full swing. He is attempting to patent not only his name and shirt number, but also the nickname 'Wor Eric' which he has acquired on Tyneside.

● A last word from 'Wor' Eric Cantona himself: 'In Newcastle I have found a faithful passion I could find with no other team in the world. Not just passion when you win, but all the time. Although when you win it's more better, obviously. And when the bloater follows the mackerel on a little dishy, it's because it thinks that the boat will soon come in. Bonny lad. Oh aye.'

Cantona is frustrated by his inability to turn up the collar on his new Newcastle shirt ... and rumours of his imminent retirement increase.

If...Graham Taylor had just had a bit of luck then... it wouldn't have been that different, really

MY CLEAREST memory of Graham Taylor as England manager is from the 1992 European Championships. He'd foolishly told the fans at home to 'sit back and watch us win it' – hubris of Ally MacLeod proportions – and, after hopelessly uninspiring goalless draws with France and Denmark, England were in serious danger of finishing bottom of their group.

With captain Gary Lineker alongside him, Taylor was doing a live-by-satellite interview, and was becoming exasperated with the questions from the experts in the UK studio.

'What do you want me to be?' he said, with his trademark barmy grin. 'Do you want me to be happy? I'll be happy. Do you want me to be sad? I'll be sad ...' And so it went on.

He was like an obliging but limited impressionist dying on his arse during a talent show.

As Lineker's smile remained fixed in place, his eyes flicked sideways warily, as if suspecting that Taylor was about to froth at the mouth and bite him.

And in homes all over the country people were shouting at the television screen, 'We want you to be unemployed!'

Taylor was appointed England manager-in-waiting before Bobby Robson took the side to Italia 90. This is the career that so impressed the FA selection panel, including of course, Peter Swales, that unerringly fine judge of a manager, whose record for successful appointments is comparable with Shane McGowan's at the dentist's.

In a new training exercise, Carlton Palmer (unseen) swings Graham Taylor round by the wrist and ankle.

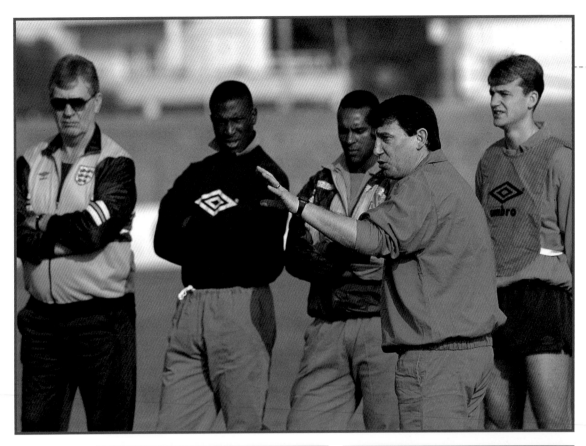

Inspirational ... Taylor made Lawrie McMenemy believe he knew about football (Above) and won the respect of Watford Chairman Elton John (Right).

GRAHAM TAYLOR MANAGERIAL ROLL OF HONOUR

1976	Lincoln City	Div 4	Champions
1978	Watford	Div 4	Champions
1979	Watford	Div 3	Runners-up
1982	Watford	Div 2	Runners-up
1983	Watford	Div 1	Runners-up
1984	Watford	FA Cup	Runners-up
1988	Aston Villa	Div 2	Runners-up
1990	Aston Villa	Div 1	Runners-up

Taylor's record looked suspiciously like that of a man who wasn't able to hold his nerve when the pressure was on, and couldn't help communicating this to his players.

Most glaringly he had tampered with the tactics that had taken Villa to the top of the League in 1990, and introduced Tony Cascarino with ten games to go, unable to resist a

return to the long-ball game. Liverpool over-hauled them. In short, he was a runner-up.

All his predecessors in the England job had taken a club to a major trophy. Ramsey won the title with Ipswich, Mercer with Manchester City. Revie won all the domestic trophies at Leeds, and the Fairs Cup too, while Greenwood and Robson had won the FA Cup with West Ham and Ipswich respectively. Howard Kendall, Taylor's main rival for the job, had also won the title, the Cup and the Cup Winners' Cup.

None the less the panel had seen how the media had torn at poor Bobby Robson, and were concerned to find a manager with good media skills. They just didn't notice that Taylor had none, and it later emerged that they'd confused him with Elton John. What Taylor did have was a puppy-like eagerness to please, and a willingness to put his head above the parapet to be shot at.

Taylor's honeymoon period with the English press was over after just one qualifying match in the build-up to Euro 92. Goals from Lineker and Beardsley took an unsettled-looking England past Poland at Wembley, but then for the second match in the group, away in Dublin, Taylor dropped Gazza to howls of protest on the back pages. A 1–1 draw scarcely vindicated the decision.

A 1–1 in the Wembley return against Eire, and two 1–0 wins over Turkey – one of those luckily scrambled via a Dennis Wise 'Hand of little Cockney yobbo' goal – left England needing a draw in Poland to qualify. They got it, Lineker equalising thirteen minutes from the end, but the manner of the achievement didn't really give much grounds for confidence.

Taylor unveiled his master plan for Sweden in his line-up for the last warm-up match, against Finland. He would play Mark Wright

Platt mesmerises McGrath with the hovering ball trick.

'Look, Graham. A goal!' Alan Smith notches against mighty Turkey.

as sweeper behind Des Walker and Martin Keown in a 1–4–3–2 formation, with John Barnes partnering Lineker up front.

Injuries picked up in that game robbed him of Barnes and Gary Stevens, who was already the third choice right-back after Lee Dixon and Rob Jones were declared unfit. UEFA allowed Taylor to make late adjustments to his squad, but strangely he replaced Barnes and Stevens with Andy Sinton, a winger, and Keith Curle, a centre-back.

When Mark Wright aggravated an Achilles tendon strain, too late for Tony Adams to be drafted in from his summer job on Blackpool beach, Taylor's planning went out of the window. He started Euro 92 with a flat back four, despite having no recognised right-back, and with Keith Curle playing there out of position against Denmark.

When this didn't work, Taylor's vacillation was painful to see. Trevor Steven was at right back against France, then David Batty had a go there against Sweden. Meanwhile Lineker, Smith, Merson, Shearer, Daley, Sinton and Platt all took a turn up front.

The crunch game was the third, against Sweden. Both teams needed to win to go through to the semi-finals, and England got a fortunate start when Platt miskicked a

Lineker cross past Thomas Ravelli for the opening goal in the third minute.

England reached half-time more or less in control, but during the break the Swedish manager made a change. Johnny Ekstrom came on for the ineffectual Anders Limpar, and within six minutes the extra pressure he put on the England defence brought an equaliser.

Taylor's response, when desperately in need of a goal, was to withdraw his captain from the fray, a man just one goal short of England's all-time goalscoring record. The move stunned the England supporters and the England team, and their morale drained away almost visibly.

Sweden took charge of the game, and deservedly won it with eight minutes to go. Afterwards Taylor was on the defensive, refusing to acknowledge his catastrophic misreading of the game and laying the blame firmly where it belonged, on the half-time break.

He was unlucky with injuries, no doubt about that, but the whole campaign was such a mismanaged horror show that it's difficult to settle on just one thing that you could change to make a significant difference, but none the less ...

If... Taylor had left Lineker on?

SIXTY-FOUR MINUTES GONE, and it's England 1, Sweden 1. Graham Taylor mutters to Lawrie McMenemy, a big man who never looked right in a tracksuit, that he is going to take Lineker off. McMenemy takes a swig from his can of Kaliber and shakes his head from side to side.

Taylor changes his mind. 'No, big man, you're right, I'll leave him on.'

McMenemy doesn't hear, however, as an insect has flown into his ear, and he continues to shake his head to try and get rid of it. Taylor, however, has moved on. 'I could take Platty off? Or what about Woodsy ...? If only Geoff Thomas were here ...'

McMenemy leans over and says, 'Here's a quiz question for you. Who won the Cup in 1976? Eh?'

Sweden continue to press, but gradually England's defenders work out how to contain Ekstrom and Brolin. Then England win a corner. The ball bounces loose in the Swedish area, Palmer lunges for it, and Lineker sweeps it into the roof of the net.

● At the post-match press conference, Taylor is grudging about his captain's achievement in equalling Bobby Charlton's long-standing England goals record. 'I thought he had a terrible match,' the manager said, 'but I know you lot think the sun shines out of his trousers so I'd better shut up.'

● The *Sun,* as it happens, unimpressed by the England performance, encapsulates

The combined football knowledge of Björk.

what it thinks in the headline 'SWEDES 1, TURNIPS 2', over a picture of a turnip with Taylor's face superimposed on it.

'Perhaps it is a little cruel,' their sports editor says, 'especially as they won the game, but since we'd thought of it, it seemed a shame not to use it.'

● England and Sweden both progress to the semi-finals, and Denmark and France are eliminated. Holland and Germany qualify from the other group, at the expense of Scotland and the CIS.

● Taylor announces his side for the semi-final against Germany in Gothenburg. The press and critics are stunned: David Platt

'No, Mr Taylor, *you've* lost you your job.'

will play at right-back, Andy Sinton at left-back, with Stuart Pearce as sweeper in a new defensive formation. Alan Smith is the lone striker, with Carlton Palmer and David Batty in behind him. Forty-nine-goal Gary Lineker is on the subs' bench, and Des Walker is captain. A famous photograph of Graham Taylor and Lawrie McMenemy with their fingers crossed appears on all the front pages.

● Germany win 6–0, with Jürgen Klinsmann scoring four. Sweden beat Holland in the other semi, and then score a popular triumph in the final.

● Gary Lineker doesn't make a substitute appearance, and ends his career level with Charlton.

BACK IN THE REAL WORLD, after Euro 92 Taylor and England embarked on the qualifying journey that they hoped would lead to USA 94. Taylor, displaying the fine judgement in media matters that had made him such an attractive choice for the FA, permitted the whole campaign to be filmed in a hilarious fly-on-the-wall documentary by Channel Four's *Cutting Edge* strand.

The camera's unforgiving lens captured

Carlton Palmer – England's playmaker.

the players' bewilderment at Taylor's incomprehensible team talks, Phil Neal's comical parroting of every thought Taylor spoke aloud, and the demise of England's chances of qualifying.

These realistically disappeared during a four-day spell which saw England playing away to Poland and Norway. They scraped a 1–1 draw thanks to sub Ian Wright in the first game. This match featured the début, courtesy of *Cutting Edge*, of Graham Taylor's odd catchphrase, 'Do I not like that!' as the Poles took the lead.

Taylor not liked it so much that for the Norway tie he made disastrous tactical changes which left the team confused and demoralised.

Out went Beardsley, Dorigo, Barnes and Ince, and Pallister was asked to play left-back in a three-man defence alongside Tony Adams and Des Walker. Norway could barely contain their mirth as they won 2–0.

Bad though this was, England still came to their penultimate qualifier, away to Holland, knowing that a draw there and a big win over San Marino would probably see them through. England could take comfort from the fact that they had bossed the Wembley encounter between the two teams until Jan Wouters had smashed Gazza's *cheekbone*.

THE TEAMS

HOLLAND
de Goey, de Wolf,
R. Koeman, F. de Boer,
Rijkaard, Wouters,
E. Koeman, Bergkamp,
Overmars (Winter), R. de
Boer (van Gobbel), Roy.

ENGLAND
Seaman, Parker, Dorigo,
Ince, Pallister, Adams, Platt,
Palmer (Sinton), Shearer,
Merson (Wright), Sharpe.

TAYLOR CLASHED volubly with journalists over his team selection for the match which took place on 13 October in Rotterdam, the papers unreasonably hoping for good players in their natural positions. Palmer was not a popular choice, and Merson was not first choice striker even at his club, Arsenal.

Holland began the game with a series of rapid attacks. Overmars skinned Dorigo repeatedly, but his crosses were wayward. Platt, Merson and Dorigo had decent chances for England, but by half-time they should have been a goal adrift.

Rijkaard had what seemed a good goal disallowed for offside, and Taylor must have begun to think it was his night. He was wrong.

Early in the second half Sinton sent Platt through on the Dutch goal, and he had the pace – ah, memories ... – to escape from the last defender, the sluggish Ronald Koeman. In desperation, Koeman grabbed at Platt and wrestled him to the ground on the edge of the area. The referee awarded a free kick and a yellow card, when a penalty and a red card would have turned the game in England's favour.

To make matters worse, Koeman scored at the other end a couple of minutes later, when he should really have been selecting perfumed bath salts.

It was a free-kick on the edge of England's area. Koeman's first, blasted, effort was charged down by Paul Ince, but the referee

Ronald Koeman is already wondering whether to take two bottles into the early shower, as Platt crashes to the ground. Unfortunately for Taylor, the ref didn't see things that way. Or at all.

ordered him to take the kick again.

Brian Moore, unusually prescient on this occasion, and recently returned from the World Subbuteo Championships, started to squeal, 'He's going to flick one now! He's going to flick one! He's going to flick one ...!', and indeed everyone watching read Koeman's mind except David Seaman, who was caught flat-footed as Koeman did indeed flick one.

Bergkamp's goal, seven minutes later,

killed England off, and the rest of the match is distinguished only by its coverage on the *Cutting Edge* documentary.

Taylor is seen remonstrating with a FIFA official about the exact dimensions of the area he is allowed to stand in.

Then he tiptoes away from the bemused young man to tell the linesman:

'The referee's got me the sack.

'Thank him ever so much for that, won't you?'

But what if...
Ronald Koeman had been sent off?

FIFTY-NINTH MINUTE. *Andy Sinton's through ball catches the Dutch defence unawares, arriving for once at a team-mate, and David Platt homes in on goal. Ronald Koeman makes a grab at the England man and hauls him to the floor. It is a clear professional foul, and the referee has no choice but to send the Dutchman off.*

In the brief mêlée following the dismissal, Ince and Rijkaard square up, and both are booked. England make a pig's ear of the free kick, but as the match wears on they gradually make their one man advantage count. Merson hits the post, as does Bergkamp at the other end – Merson with his head, Bergkamp with the ball.

HOLLAND	**0**
ENGLAND	**0**

● This leaves Holland and England level on twelve points behind Norway (sixteen points) and one game to play. Holland travel to Poland, while England go to San Marino. If Holland win, then England need to better their margin of victory by five to qualify.

● The task is made all the harder by Davide Gualtieri's eighth-second opening goal for San Marino, but goals from Ince (2), Wright (4) and Ferdinand give England a comfortable 7–1 win, and they anxiously wait for news from Poland. The Dutch have been nervous, apprehensive, and unsettled by the undulating terrain and lack of bikes. They only managed a 1–1 draw, so Taylor has qualified for USA 94 by the skin of his teeth.

● England's qualification leads Graham Taylor to treat the *Cutting Edge* documentary as a bit of good-natured fun. He allows his picture to be used on an instructive Boy Scout leaflet entitled 'Do I Knot Like That?', and appears with Trev and Simon on *Going Live* to pronounce his opinion on current boy bands. 'Do I not like Take That!' he cries to squeals of approval from teenage girls in the audience, who don't understand what he's said but know he's said the words Take That.

● Taylor trademarks his phrase so no one else can use it. So Richard Little-john's late-night sports bearpit is entitled *The Fat Fool talks Football*.

Friday, June 4, 1993   3X

The vegetable stall is back in business

YOU'VE GONE AND DUNG IT AGAIN, TAYLOR...

Sun
NORSE MANURE
From later editions of yesterday's Sun

ENGLAND manager Graham Taylor dropped us all in the Norse manure with the shambles of a side he put out against Norway.

And yesterday The Sun's army of readers delivered their verdict on Turnip Taylor, who has wrecked our hopes of going to the United States next year to compete in the World Cup finals.

SUNSPORT SAYS

With one voice they called for his head.

Not when he wants to go. Not when the stuffed shirts at the FA finally get round to giving him the shove. But NOW.

Taylor has lost the plot. His players were like passing strangers as they crashed 2-0 on Wednesday night. The Norwegians — hardly a world soccer force with a pedigree like the Brazilians — knew they would win before a ball was kicked.

Taylor admits he has no idea why his side played without passion or pride. But is he going to do the decent thing and chuck it in? Not on your life.

Incredibly, he got the sup-port of his boss, Peter Swales, chairman of the FA's international committee.

He said: "Why should he go? We can still qualify for the World Cup finals."

In your dreams, Swales, in your dreams.

And only if you ditch the man who has turned our national side into a nightmare.

Taylor's media skills were a positive boon in his relationships with the press.

Taylor's trademark is called into question only once, by Susan Hampshire, but this turns out to be a mostike.

● In the USA England are dispatched to Florida to play in Group F along with Belgium, Saudi Arabia and Morocco. Taylor plays a sweeper system against Belgium, and England lose 3–0. He sends out a team with four left wingers against Saudi Arabia – the surprise package of the World Cup – and England lose 3–0 again.

● The headline in the *Sun* is 'SAUNDLI BEATEN', and underneath they apologise for not being able to think of anything better on account of being too depressed. In his post-

match press conference Taylor claims to be enjoying the tournament. 'They've got McDonald's here, you know.' he chirps.

● Taylor faces a player revolt before the Morocco game, and the team is rumoured to have been selected by David Platt. England win 2–0, but the two points are not enough to take them through to the second phase.

● Graham Taylor resigns on his return to the UK. He is offered the job of Wolves manager, but says he wishes to take a long break from football. Like England have for the last four years. Ian Branfoot takes over at Molineux, and Wolves are promoted at the end of 1994–5 as champions.

If... Mark Hughes hadn't got that last minute volley then... Ryan Giggs would be a matador

RARELY CAN A GOAL have had such a dramatic impact as the stunning – or shattering, depending on your point of view – volley with which Mark Hughes hauled Manchester United back from the brink of defeat in the 1994 FA Cup semi-final.

With one smashing strike the curly-topped Welshman saved not only United's Cup run, but their entire season.

It had all seemed to be going so smoothly for the red machine, as they moved inexorably towards the first-ever Treble in English football. Their feathers were ruffled by Galatasaray in a bad-tempered exit from the European Cup, but in domestic football they were unbeaten for thirty-four matches between a defeat by Chelsea in September and another defeat by Chelsea in the return match in March.

Then, however, the wheels started to come off United's ugly and ostentatious vehicle, big style. Schmeichel was sent off in the Cup quarter final against Charlton for a foul that was practically in the opponents' half. Cantona was dismissed for stamping on John Moncur at Swindon, and then again at Highbury three days later.

Then Aston Villa put paid to the Treble, taking the Coca-Cola Cup with a fine 3–1 win at Wembley, goals by Dalian Atkinson and Dean Saunders (2). For good measure, Andrei Kanchelskis, their influential Ukrainian, was red-carded for deliberate handball in the last minute of the match.

When Blackburn Rovers, who had been sixteen points adrift only a couple of months earlier, narrowed United's lead at the top of the table to just three with a Shearer-inspired win at Ewood Park, it began to look as though United's bottle had gone. The possibility that United might end up with nothing was touted delightedly up and down the land – except in the United strongholds, Cornwall and Essex – as they prepared for the FA Cup semi against Oldham, wondering

Sparky minus *that* piano.

Bryan Robson is an inspiration to all youngsters.

if they could find eleven players whose disciplinary records would permit them to play.

Oldham Athletic, meanwhile, had spent the whole season nervously eyeing the drop zone at the other end of the table. The previous season they had scrambled clear only by winning their final three games in eight days, by the way handing the title to Manchester United with an unexpected victory at Villa Park.

Latics reached January stuck in the bottom three, but with plenty of teams still in trouble just above them.

The desperate trawl for League points meant that they reached the quarter final of the FA Cup before they really realised they had a Cup run going, scrappy single goal wins over Derby, Stoke and Barnsley bringing them a sexy tie against fashionable local rivals Bolton.

Bolton's high-profile progress had accounted for Everton, Arsenal, and Aston Villa, and they were clear favourites, but a Darren Beckford steal six minutes from time took Oldham through.

As they tiptoed through the Cup Oldham's League form picked up, and when they met Manchester United at Old Trafford six days before their Wembley date they were in better form than the faltering champions. Five wins in the previous eight games had taken Athletic to within touching distance of safety, and they played with freedom and vigour to rattle United before going down 3–2.

The day before the United–Oldham semi, Chelsea beat a Luton side unable to come to terms with being known as 'The Hatters' to reach the final.

THE TEAMS

MANCHESTER UNITED
Schmeichel, Parker (Butt), Irwin, Bruce, Sharpe, Pallister, McClair, Ince, Dublin (Robson), Hughes, Giggs.

OLDHAM ATHLETIC
Hallworth, Makin, Pointon, Henry, Jobson, Fleming, Bernard, Beckford, Sharp, Milligan, Holden.

Paul Bernard
leaves Paul Ince
in his wake.

N 1990 UNITED and Oldham had played a thrilling semi-final at Maine Road, with both sides holding the lead before sharing the honours in a 3–3 draw. The 1994 game was, in stark contrast, a dour, mistake-ridden affair played at Wembley on 10 April. There were complaints about this choice of venue from Manchester United fans, some of whomboycotted the game in protest, but these were ignored by the FA on the grounds that they'd make more dosh, and most of the United fans would only be making a short tube journey in any case.

It was extra time before the deadlock was broken. Schmeichel – perhaps temporarily dazzled by the luminosity of his own konk – flapped uselessly at a corner, and the ball fell

Neil Pointon scores as Bryan Robson hails a passing taxi.

to Oldham full-back Neil Pointon, who was one of the last advocates with Ian Marshall of the genuine seventies footballer's hairdo. Pointon whacked the ball into the net, and United's season seemed in ruins, shattered by a goal from Leo Sayer's double.

The last minutes ticked away, with Oldham defending resolutely along the edge of their area. Finally, with seconds only remaining, Butt and McClair nodded the ball hopefully forward, and Hughes caught it just right on the volley. The ball fizzed past Hallworth, and Fleming, who had marked Hughes expertly for 119 minutes and fifteen seconds, gaped in disbelief.

This one thrilling moment revitalised United and shattered Oldham. And not just for the next few minutes. Oldham got whacked 4–1 in the replay, with Kanchelskis returning from suspension to be man of the match. Once again Pointon was Oldham's goalscorer, and these two were his only goals of the season. Worth noting by managers, that: United defenders are distracted by perms.

United surged on to the double. In the League they regained their confidence and form, winning four straight matches to leave Blackburn eight points behind. Chelsea succumbed 4–0 in the Cup final, with Cantona claiming two penalties.

Oldham, on the other hand, were destroyed. From a position of comparative security in the League they fell away to be relegated second from bottom. If they had taken just six points

from their last eight games they'd have been safe, but they managed only three.

The following season manager Joe Royle lost interest. During his twelve-year tenure at Boundary Park he had been repeatedly linked with larger clubs, and in November he finally accepted the Everton job. Graeme Sharp took over, and the top players jumped ship. Paul Bernard, Paul Gerrard, Gunnar Halle and Mike Milligan found new higher profile clubs, and Richard Jobson left to reform The Skids.

Gates fell away dramatically, and three years later Athletic were relegated again. The sole consolation was that for the first time in three years they didn't have the most shit ground in their division.

Pointon just can't stop scoring.

But what if... Hughes had not scored that goal?

THE DYING SECONDS, Oldham 1–0 up. The United players playing head tennis on the edge of the area. The ball drops for Mark Hughes, one of the best volleyers in the game. On this occasion, however, he slices it high and wide and it bounces harmlessly on to the running track.

United heads fall, and the Oldham players are in no hurry to get the ball back into play. As Hallworth punts the goal kick upfield the referee blows for full-time, and Hughes trudges dejectedly from the field while Pointon – but not his hair – disappears under a mountain of blue-shirted team-mates. Ferguson and Brian Kidd point at their watches, which are very nice.

The Cup final, Oldham Athletic v Chelsea. Oldham have beaten Chelsea home and away in the League this season, and their winning streak over the Londoners continues. Sub Andy Ritchie scores the only goal, and Mike Milligan lifts the Cup.

● The win in the semi gives Oldham the psychological lift they need to secure Premiership football for 1994–5 with something to spare, and Ipswich are relegated with Sheffield United and Swindon Town. Manchester United, however, fall away badly, and Blackburn catch them at the last to win the League title and leave Old Trafford's trophy cabinet bare. Alan Shearer is Footballer of the Year.

● Martin Edwards is upbeat. 'Football is a business,' he says, 'and look what we've saved on Duraglit.'

● Alex Ferguson is left fuming by United's collapse, and begins a mass clear-out of those players he says haven't the guts to play for him. Peter Schmeichel goes to Liverpool where he alternates with David James. Bruce Grobbelaar organises a book on which of them will drop the most corners at forwards' feet in the season.

● Steve Bruce goes to Tranmere, Gary Pallister to Arsenal to help remedy their big slow centre-half shortage, Roy Keane to Blackburn to replace the injured David Batty. Paul Ince moves to Celtic, Mark Hughes to Feyenoord, Ryan Giggs to Barcelona and Denis Irwin returns to Oldham. Eric Cantona is so affronted by Ferguson's willingness to listen to offers for him that he retires and sets up in business writing the little poems that go inside birthday cards.

Andrei Kanchelskis,
captaincy material.

Andy Ritchie's last-minute shot beats David Seaman to win the Cup Winners' Cup for Oldham Athletic.

● By the time Ferguson calms down and realises what he's done it is too late, and he opens his campaign with Andrei Kanchelskis as his new club captain. He tries to strengthen his squad, but other managers will not release their best players to United. Ferguson gets very steamed up about this, and about the issue of releasing players for international duty. He wants to refuse to do this, but it is gently pointed out to him that he has hardly any internationals left. He signs Cyrille Regis in a bid to start a row with the French Guyana FA. Regis has to tell him he played for England.

● The mid-season capture of Andy Cole is not enough to prevent United from having a 'transitional season', and they finish nineteenth. Alan Hansen professes himself surprised that United's youngsters didn't do better, saying, 'I thought you could win everything with kids.'

● Everton have a poor start to the following season, and in November they sack manager Mike Walker. Joe Royle turns down their overtures as Oldham are still in the Cup Winners' Cup after their two-leg win over Viktoria Zizkov. Everton approach, and are turned down by, Johan Cruyff, Bobby Robson, Terry Venables, Peter Reid, Brian Horton, Kevin Keegan, Dave Bassett, Colin Murphy, Alan Ball, Ian Greaves, Graham Taylor, John Bond, Peter Withe and Malcolm MacDonald, although Phil Neal is interested and gets his application in early. Everton call in a sewage expert to see if there's a nasty smell about the place that they've all got used to. He says there is, and eventually Brian Labone's socks are found behind a radiator. Finally they ring Notts County to see if anyone there knows Howard Kendall's phone number.

● Blackburn win the League again, ahead of nearest rivals Liverpool, while the Cup final is an all-London affair between Crystal Palace and Spurs. Spurs clinch it with a Jürgen Klinsmann penalty, awarded when Jürgen Klinsmann stumbled over the outstretched leg of Jürgen Klinsmann. Alan Sugar grabs the prize of Klinsmann's Cup final shirt, joking, 'I'm going to go and wash my car with this now!'

● Oldham and Joe Royle have their best season in the Premiership, finishing ninth. They also reach the final of the Cup Winners' Cup, where a speculative shot by Andy Ritchie from the halfway line in the last minute catches David Seaman off his line and wins the all-English Euro-clash with holders Arsenal.

● After Blackburn sell Alan Shearer to Newcastle the Geordies become the dominant force in English football, the team everyone has to beat, the 1996 champions. With Manchester United languishing in their transitional period still, Newcastle's crowds and merchandising machine are the envy of the country.

● Ferguson is generous in his praise of Keegan's team. 'They're c**p', he says as he clears his desk at Old Trafford. He becomes manager of Wales, and finds he cannot get Ryan Giggs released by Barcelona for any of his first twelve games in charge, owing to groin strains, head-colds, calf niggles, paella poisoning, wrist injuries picked up during matador training, etc, etc.

If...

Southgate had scored then... Paul Ince would love pizza

I SUPPOSE MOST OF US knew what was coming. We hoped for the best when Shearer put England ahead after a couple of minutes, hoped for a performance like the one which had swept the Dutch aside, but once Kuntz had equalised it always felt like it would be penalties again.

And the Germans always win when it goes to penalties.

Euro 96 had begun under a cloud. Terry Venables had taken his extended squad to the Far East for a controversial warm-up tour and although England won both games against China and a Hong Kong Golden XI, the papers were full of pictures of players getting pissed up and descriptions of an arrangement known as 'the Dentist's Chair'. This involved the players taking it in turns to lie back and have tequila poured down them.

Then Cathay Pacific claimed that players continued the party on the flight home and caused £5,000 worth of damage to their air-craft. Some busybody MPs demanded that the players responsible be dropped from the tournament. In response, the squad issued a statement declining to identify the guilty men, operating a system of collective responsibility, although Steve McManaman and Robbie Fowler said it wasn't them.

The tournament began with one of those excruciating opening ceremonies, devised by the sort of people who were pleased when the Younger Generation interrupted *The Two Ronnies*. It featured some dancing that was even ropier than that paraded by the Sky Strikers, and an incomprehensible sequence of blokes riding around in armour.

To top it all off there was a display of national flags that could only be appreciated from an airship.

Oh, and there was a match, as well, in which England drew 1–1 with Switzerland. This was England's first opportunity to assess the international managership of Terry Venables, after two years of inconse-

Southgate: why didn't he just whack it?

Gascoigne solves his 'refuelling' problems.

quential friendlies, and it didn't bode that well. Shearer ended his long-standing scoring drought, which was good, but Terry took McManaman off when he was our best player, which was bad.

Scotland had a gutsy 0–0 draw with Holland under their belts when they came to play England, and for the first half looked strong and capable of getting a result. At half-time, though, Venables brought on Redknapp and switched McManaman to the right side, where he combined with Neville to make a smashing goal for Shearer.

Scotland were awarded a penalty when Adams brought down Durie, but Seaman stopped McAllister's kick with an elbow, and straight away England scored again. Gascoigne received from Anderton, flicked the ball over Hendry, and volleyed it as it dropped low past Goram.

Gascoigne knew he'd done something special – a goal like that could keep him in the side through at least six shite performances and eight months on the piss. In his delight he assumed the Dentist's Chair position, and his mates squirted water in his mouth. At least I think it was water.

Then came a memorable thrashing of Holland. Shearer and Sheringham both scored twice as England overwhelmed the dangerous Dutch, and Wembley echoed to Baddiel and Skinner's annoyingly catchy anthem, 'Felines On The Shirt'.

Spain had the better of the quarter final, having one perfectly good goal disallowed, but England came through after a stomach-churning introduction to 'Golden goal' extra time, and a penalty shoot out. Hierro missed for Spain, and Seaman saved from Nadal, while England's four penalties were emphatic.

Stuart Pearce, who slammed home the third to atone for the miss of Italia 90, received the loudest cheer of all, perhaps partly because he looked prepared to smack anyone who wasn't pleased for him. Venables, in an unusual post-match interview, announced that he had 'singed the King of Spain's beard'. In the meantime Germany had been making inexorable progress to the semi-final. They beat the Czechs 2–0, and the Russians 3–0, before sharing the goalless draw which sent their opponents Italy home early. They then came through a bruising quarter final with Croatia 2–1.

Stuart Pearce struggles to pronounce the name of the Spanish keeper.

THE TEAMS

ENGLAND
Seaman, Southgate, Pearce, Adams, Platt, Ince, Anderton, McManaman, Gascoigne, Sheringham, Shearer.

GERMANY
Kopke, Sammer, Reuter, Babbel, Helmer (Bode), Ziege, Scholl (Hassler), Freund (Strunz), Moller, Eilts, Kuntz.

THE EURO 96 semi-final, 26 June, Wembley. Adams flicked on Gascoigne's second minute corner, and Shearer slipped in to nod home. For fifteen minutes England fans almost allowed themselves to believe that this time it would be different, but shades of Italia 90 loomed ever larger from the moment Kuntz pulled the Germans level.

The Germans took the first half on points, England the second, in a classic match. Ince and Gazza went close, and Eilts for the Germans was a formidable opponent in defence. Barry Davies attempted to pay tribute to him, saying, 'There's Dieter Eilts, built like a brick... door ...'

Now, it sort of makes sense, a brick door, but surely Barry got two proverbial things confused there. Either Dieter Eilts is built like a brick shithouse, or he bangs like a shithouse door. Whichever it is, the key word, as I'm sure you'll agree, is shithouse.

In a nerve-shredding period of 'golden goal' extra time Anderton hit a post, and Gazza was a split second late lunging at a cross a couple of yards out, while Germany, heartstoppingly, had a goal ruled out.

Shearer gives England the dream start before Kuntz's wake-up call.

Andreas Moller (Germany).

And then it was penalties, and the Germans always win when it goes to penalties.

Shearer for England, Hassler for Germany. Platt for England, Strunz for Germany. Pearce exorcising another ghost of Italia 90 for England, Reuter, another Italia 90 veteran, for Germany. Gascoigne matched by Ziege, Sheringham cancelled out by Kuntz.

Then it became apparent that events had exhausted Venables' planning, and no one was sure who should take England's sixth. Ince looked away, McManaman shrugged, Gareth Southgate stepped forward. He was one of England's finds of the tournament, but he'd only ever taken one penalty before, while at Crystal Palace, and he'd missed that.

He missed this one as well, stroking it too carefully and obviously to Kopke's right, the goalkeeper pushing it away. Moller – a German Stan Boardman lookalike – strode up and blasted Germany's sixth, and then swaggered off to receive the congratulations of his chums.

England's roller-coaster ride was over, and so was the stewardship of Terry Venables, who was resigning to spend more time with his lawyers.

Germany beat the Czech Republic in the final with a 'golden goal'.

But what if...
Southgate had scored?

FIVE–FIVE, SOUTHGATE STEPS UP to take the next penalty. As he paces his short run-up he remembers his mother's advice, 'If you get a penalty, our Gareth, just whack it!' Gareth does just that, past Andreas Kopke's despairing grasp. 6–5.

Moller steps up and smashes in Germany's next. 6–6.

Paul Ince, the self-styled 'Guv'nor', is finally persuaded that there is some guv'-ning to do, and he will take the seventh. He opts for power rather than placement, and crashes the ball against the bar with Kopke nowhere. The ball rockets downwards on or about the goal line, and out. Ince claims the goal, but the linesman says 'No'. In the crowd, Roger Hunt and Bobby Charlton turn away, convinced it is over the line, but despite protests the goal is not given. Television pictures are inconclusive, Ince is furious.

Strunz scores the seventh for Germany, Seaman getting a hand to it but unable to keep it out.

The Germans always win when it goes to penalties.

The England bench congratulate Gareth – a disappointed Pizza Hut exec looks on.

indignantly claims Ince's penalty was good. 'It's 1996 all over again,' he cries.

● Dorinel Munteanu, the Romanian whose 'goal' against Bulgaria was disallowed when it had clearly bounced down over the line,

● Paul Ince makes £100,000 promoting Pizza Hut in adverts with Stuart Pearce and Chris Waddle.

Picture credits

Allsport – pages 7, 8, 14, 16, 25, 27, 30, 31, 33, 35, 48, 51, 53, 54, 55, 57, 59, 63, 81, 82, 83, 84, 85, 86, 89, 91, 94, 95, 97, 100, 101, 102,108, 109, 118, 125, 126, 127, 134, 136, 138, 139, 141, 146, 147, 148, 149, 151, 152, 155, 156, 157, 158, 159
Ardea – page 9
BBC – page 127
Colorsport – pages 29, 34, 38, 55, 56, 103, 123, 124, 133, 137, 158
Football Archives – pages 11, 18, 50, 52
Hulton Getty – page 117
Tristram Kenton – page 114
Mark Leech – pages 36, 65
Mike Maloney – page 26
MSI – pages 6, 15, 42, 134
PA Photos – page 13
Popperfoto – pages 28, 29, 32, 37, 40, 41, 47, 58, 59, 64, 67, 78, 87, 99, 107, 111, 113, 120, 121, 128, 131, 145
Rex Features – pages 23, 61, 98, 104, 124
Sportsphoto – page 129
Ron Vavasour – page 39
A.C. Weedon – page 20

The Publishers would like to thank the Corner House, Manchester, for their assistance.

The authors and publishers have made every reasonable effort to contact all copyright holders. Any errors that may have occurred are inadvertent and anyone who for any reason has not been contacted is invited to write to the publishers so that a full acknowledgement may be made in subsequent editions of this work.